Queluz

Queluz

THE PALACE AND GARDENS

Maria Inês Ferro

M|C
MINISTÉRIO DA CULTURA

IPPAR
INSTITUTO PORTUGUÊS
DO PATRIMÓNIO
ARQUITECTÓNICO

Scala Books

ACKNOWLEDGEMENTS

Our thanks to Paulo Pereira at IPPAR (the Portuguese Institute for Architectural Heritage), who from the beginning committed himself to creating this book, to Iria Caetano for her support in its co-ordination and to Dulce Freitas Ferraz whose task was to organize the mass of scattered photographic material.

Our thanks go also to the entire team at the National Palace of Queluz and in particular, Teresa Cancela Vilaça and Maria da Conceição Coelho for their assistance in documentary archive research and technical support. The family tree was created by Teresa Cancela Vilaça and Isabel Jacinto Nunes.

First published in 1997 by Scala Publishers Ltd
Gloucester Mansions
140a Shaftesbury Avenue
LONDON WC2H 8HD

1997 1st Edition
All Rights Reserved

Reprinted in 2002

Designed by Peter Ling
Edited by Tim Ayers
Printed and bound in Spain by
G. Z. Printek, S.A.L., Zamudio

ISBN 1 85759 174 7 (hardback)
ISBN 927-8087-40-3 (paperback)

Photographic credits
Luís Pavão: pp 13, 16, 17, 18, 19, 20, 24, 25, 26, 27, 28, 29, 30, 38, 41, 43, ,54, 56, 57, 58, 59, 60, 61, 63, 64, 67, 68, 69, 70, 71, 72, 73, 74, 76, 77, 78, 79, 80, 81, 82, 83, 85, 86, 87, 88, 91, 92, 94, 95, 96, 97, 98, 99, 100, 101, 102, 104, 105, 106, 109, 113, 115, 117, 123, 125
Henrique Ruas: pp 21, 22, 25, 35, 36, 47, 65, 73, 102, 107, 112, 114, 118, 120, 122
Laura Castro Caldas/Paulo Cintra: pp 12, 15, 30, 34, 37, 39, 40, 45, 50, 51, 65, 116,
João Poppe: pp 23, 31, 118
José Pessoa: pp 32, 44, 46, 48, 124
Nicolas Sapieha: pp 106, 108, 109, 110, 119
PH3, Fotografia Audio Visuais, Lda.: p 14
Francisco Matias: p 42
Alfa: p 52
Vitor Branco: p 62
Ezequiel Santos: p 66
Direcção Geral dos Edificios e Monumentos Nacionais (DGEMN): pp 25, 73.

Foreword

Amongst the royal palaces of Portugal, Queluz occupies a special place. Within this restful estate at the gateway to Lisbon, yet at the same time far removed from the duties of court life, the splendours of an elegant and carefree way of life were frittered away during a period of history that witnessed the destruction of Lisbon by the earthquake in 1755 and the eventful flight of the Portuguese royal family to Brazil in 1807.

The scenario could not have been more appropriate. The old house had become a magnificent residence of generous proportions, with the most outstanding examples of contemporary artifice used to great effect. The unity of the various buildings is remarkable: a well-structured rocaille language punctuates the fountains and gardens whilst the interior is invaded by whimsical ornamentation in gilt carving, serving as a worthy setting for the superb collections of eighteenth century furniture, paintings, porcelain and other works in gold.

IPPAR has always been concerned with the systematic defence of heritage, and as the historic palace at Queluz is now 250 years old, IPPAR has decided to publish this comprehensive guide to the interiors of the palace and its extensive gardens. This is the beginning of a series of titles that will endure for posterity, further enhanced by the establishment, for the first time, of a partnership with a major publishing house on the international scene.

Our historic initiative has succeeded, combining the precisely drawn description of this unique royal household with a profound reflection on the position of the estate, the Palace and its wonderful decorative contents in Portuguese history.

Luís Ferreira Calado
President of IPPAR

Contents

PLAN OF THE GARDENS

1 Robillion Staircase or Lion Staircase
2 Shell-work Cascade
3 Cages for Exotic Animals
4 Tile Canal in the Jamor stream
5 Sculpture of *Samson killing a Philistine* by John Cheere.
6 Medallion Lake
7 Neptune Lake, (from Quinta do Senhor da Serra in Belas) by Ercole Ferrata and Lorenzo Bernini, attributed to Bernini school
8a) Queen D. Amélia's Stables
8b) Portuguese School of Equestrian Art
9 Tea Pavilion
10 Quoits Corner or "Jogo da Pela"
11 New open-air Riding School where the Portuguese School of Equestrian Art exhibits *haute école*
12 Great Cascade
13 Shell-work Lake
14 The Horse Gateway, portraying the winged horse Pegasus bearing Fame
15 Pensile Garden
16 The Garden of Malta
17 Ajuda Gateway

N

S

PLAN OF THE PALACE

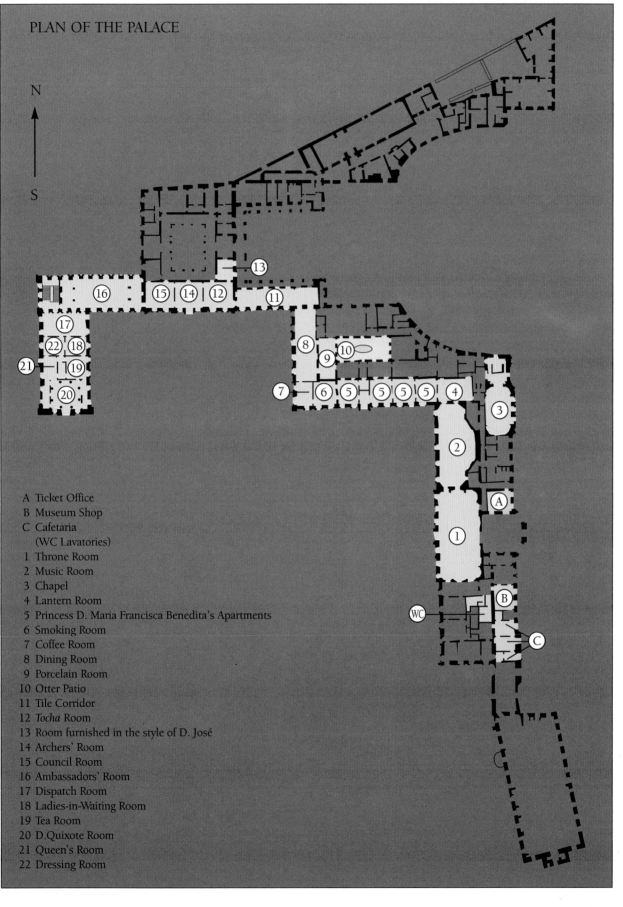

A Ticket Office
B Museum Shop
C Cafetaria
   (WC Lavatories)
1 Throne Room
2 Music Room
3 Chapel
4 Lantern Room
5 Princess D. Maria Francisca Benedita's Apartments
6 Smoking Room
7 Coffee Room
8 Dining Room
9 Porcelain Room
10 Otter Patio
11 Tile Corridor
12 *Tocha* Room
13 Room furnished in the style of D. José
14 Archers' Room
15 Council Room
16 Ambassadors' Room
17 Dispatch Room
18 Ladies-in-Waiting Room
19 Tea Room
20 D.Quixote Room
21 Queen's Room
22 Dressing Room

THE ROYAL FAMILY TREE

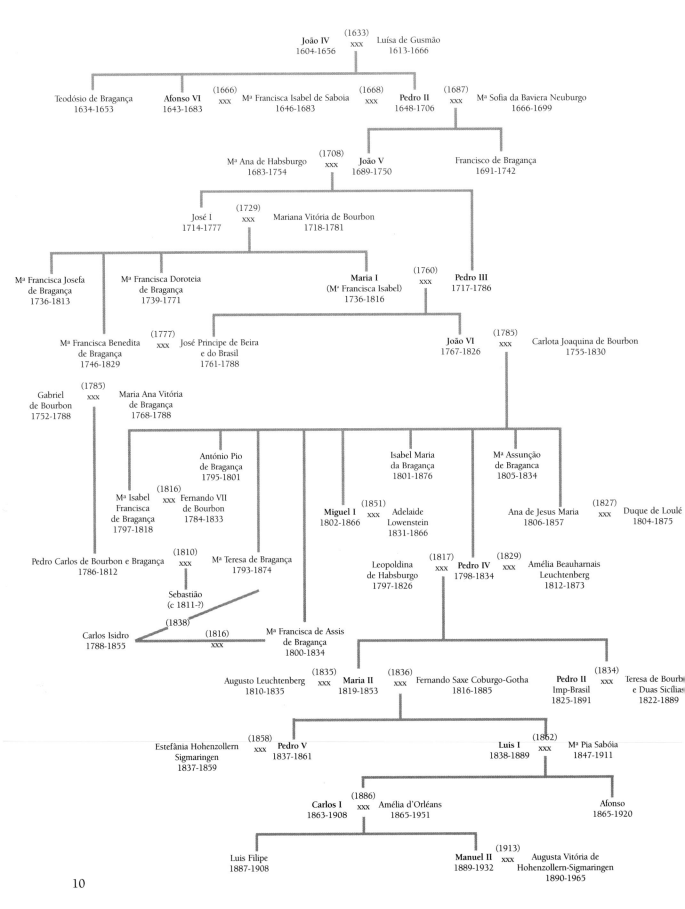

João IV (1633) Luísa de Gusmão
1604-1656 xxx 1613-1666

Teodósio de Bragança 1634-1653   **Afonso VI** 1643-1683   (1666) xxx Mª Francisca Isabel de Saboia 1646-1683   (1668) xxx **Pedro II** 1648-1706   (1687) xxx Mª Sofia da Baviera Neuburgo 1666-1699

Mª Ana de Habsburgo 1683-1754   (1708) xxx **João V** 1689-1750   Francisco de Bragança 1691-1742

José I 1714-1777   (1729) xxx Mariana Vitória de Bourbon 1718-1781

Mª Francisca Josefa de Bragança 1736-1813   Mª Francisca Doroteia de Bragança 1739-1771   **Maria I** (Mª Francisca Isabel) 1736-1816   (1760) xxx **Pedro III** 1717-1786

Mª Francisca Benedita de Bragança 1746-1829   (1777) xxx José Principe de Beira e do Brasil 1761-1788   **João VI** 1767-1826   (1785) xxx Carlota Joaquina de Bourbon 1755-1830

Gabriel de Bourbon 1752-1788   (1785) xxx Maria Ana Vitória de Bragança 1768-1788

António Pio de Bragança 1795-1801   Isabel Maria da Bragança 1801-1876   Mª Assunção de Bragança 1805-1834

Mª Isabel Francisca de Bragança 1797-1818   (1816) xxx Fernando VII de Bourbon 1784-1833   **Miguel I** 1802-1866   (1851) xxx Adelaide Lowenstein 1831-1866   Ana de Jesus Maria 1806-1857   (1827) xxx Duque de Loulé 1804-1875

Pedro Carlos de Bourbon e Bragança 1786-1812   (1810) xxx Mª Teresa de Bragança 1793-1874   Leopoldina de Habsburgo 1797-1826   (1817) xxx **Pedro IV** 1798-1834   (1829) xxx Amélia Beauharnais Leuchtenberg 1812-1873

Sebastião (c 1811-?)

Carlos Isidro 1788-1855   (1838)   (1816) xxx Mª Francisca de Assis de Bragança 1800-1834

Augusto Leuchtenberg 1810-1835   (1835) xxx **Maria II** 1819-1853   (1836) xxx Fernando Saxe Coburgo-Gotha 1816-1885   **Pedro II** Imp-Brasil 1825-1891   (1834) xxx Teresa de Bourb e Duas Sicílias 1822-1889

Estefânia Hohenzollern Sigmaringen 1837-1859   (1858) xxx **Pedro V** 1837-1861   **Luis I** 1838-1889   (1862) xxx Mª Pia Sabóia 1847-1911

Carlos I 1863-1908   (1886) xxx Amélia d'Orléans 1865-1951   Afonso 1865-1920

Luis Filipe 1887-1908   **Manuel II** 1889-1932   (1913) xxx Augusta Vitória de Hohenzollern-Sigmaringen 1890-1965

CONSTRUCTION PHASES

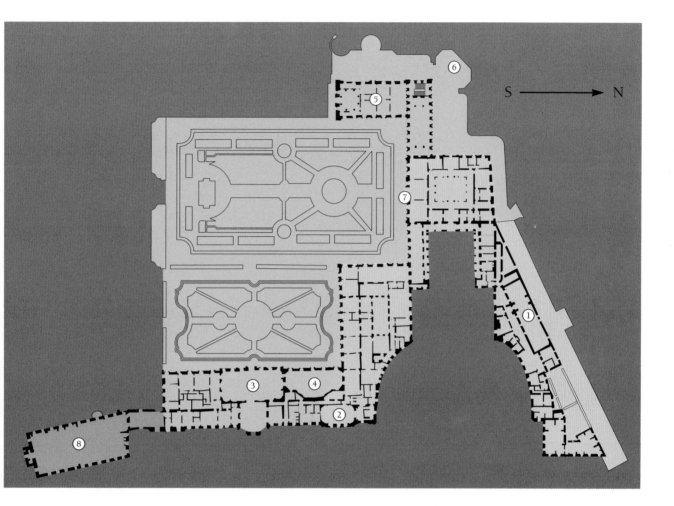

S ──────▶ N

Original centre of the Palace. Site of the *palacete* belonging to the Marquis of Castelo Rodrigo (1) which was completed in the 16th century. Its ruins were demolished in 1939 and all that remains are the vaulted cellars. .

First Construction Phase (1747-1758) – supervised by architect Mateus Vicente de Oliveira. Started by Dom Pedro (the future King Pedro III) on the country house at Queluz. Adaptation of the former palace of the Marquis of Castelo Rodrigo; construction of the chapel wing (2) and the wing containing the future Throne Room (3) and the Music Room (4).

Second Construction Phase (1760-1786) – supervised by the French architect Jean-Baptiste Robillion. Redecoration of the Music Room and the Throne Room under the supervision of Mateus Vicente de Oliveira. Robillion was responsible for the construction and decoration of the interior of the west wing, the Robillion Pavilion (5), the Robillion Staircase (6), the Facade of Ceremonies (7) and the garden layout.

Third Construction Phase (1786-1792) – supervised by the architect Manuel Caetano de Sousa. Construction of the Dona Maria Pavilion (8), situated on the site of the former Opera House, which was demolished. Now the residence for visiting foreign heads of state.

Construction

Stages & Architects

FROM THE CASTELO RODRIGO TO THE CASA DO INFANTADO

Situated about 12 km from Lisbon, on the road to Sintra, the Palace of Queluz owes its existence to the initiative of King Pedro (1717–1786), to whom the estate known as the Quinta de Queluz belonged, in his capacity as third Lord of the Estate of the Household of the Infante. The Estate had been established in 1654 by a Royal Charter of João IV, in favour of the second sons of the Kings of Portugal. It included all property confiscated after the Restoration and ascension to the throne of the Duke of Braganza from sympathizers with the Castilian Spanish, who had ruled Portugal for the past sixty years (1580–1640).

Down the centuries, the land and houses in the small town of Queluz had belonged to various landowners and there is already a mention of 'Queylus' in a judgement issued during the reign of King Afonso IV (1325–1357). During the third quarter of the sixteenth century, the lands were in the hands of Dona Margarida Corte Real, who married in 1581 Dom Cristóvão de Moura (1538–1613); the couple entailed the property upon their son, Manuel de Moura Corte Real (1592–1652), 1st Count of Lumiares and 2nd Marquis of Castelo Rodrigo, who took it over in 1613. The ruined Palace of Cristóvão de Moura, as it was known, was demolished in 1939, but photographs of it survive.

Accused of treason for his actions during the period of the Spanish occupation (he and his father had been supporters of the dynasty of the Filipes), Dom Manuel de Moura had his property confiscated in 1642. When King João created the *Casa do Infantado*,

Opposite: King Pedro III. By an unknown painter, 3rd quarter of the 18th century. Oil on canvas, 1550 x 1070 mm.
(National Palace of Queluz)

Right: Dom Cristóvão de Moura, 1st Marquis of Castelo Rodrigo, in an engraving, Antwerp, 17th century. 280 x 196 mm.
(National Palace of Queluz)

on 11 August 1654, he included within it the Quinta de Queluz, which came to be given to the Infante Dom Pedro (1648-1706), first Lord of the Estate, who used it as his summer residence.

In Lisbon, Dom Pedro lived in the Palace of the Cortes Reais (Royal Courts), also known as the Palace of Corpo Santo, birthplace of the Infante Dom Francisco (1691-1742), second Lord of the same *Casa do Infantado*. Dom Francisco, who spent time hunting at Queluz, during the summer months especially, carried out extensions to the building under the direction of the architect Manuel da Costa Negreiros (d. 1750), including the building of a chapel and small tower (later demolished), as well as the aqueduct that still exists today and various other constructions for collecting water. This Infante, however, had something of

a reputation amongst the local people, who did not dare leave their homes, afraid of his cruel and whimsical nature. It was said that one of his favourite pastimes was to indulge in target practice, aiming at sailors who were hung from the masts of ships moored in the River Tagus.

Above: Infante Dom Francisco, 2nd Lord of the Estate of the Household of the Infante. Attributed to Giorgio Domenico Duprá, c. 1729–30. Oil on canvas, 1220 x 900 mm. (C.P.)

Opposite: Infanta Dona Maria Francisca Isabel (Queen Maria I). Attributed to Francisco Vieira Lusitano, c. 1753. Oil on canvas, 1520 x 1070 mm. (National Palace of Queluz)

PEDRO III, THE GREAT BUILDER

King Pedro III (1717–1786), youngest son of King João V (1680–1750) and Mariana of Austria (1683–1754), Prior of Crato, Prince of Brazil and Lord of the Estate of the Infante at the age of 25, began a concerted building programme at Queluz between 1747 and 1786, extending the Old Palace and giving it, in time, the title of Royal Palace.

The determining factor in this was his marriage in 1760 to his niece and the heiress to the throne, Princess Maria, which brought him the crown as King Pedro III. Until the end of the eighteenth century, Queluz underwent successive enlargements and changes, according to the requirements of the Royal Family. However, it always retained its character as a summer residence, a haven from Court routine and protocol, offering from the beginning an all-pervading closeness with the gardens that were overlooked by the main façades of the building. Departing from the Pombaline style then prevalent in Lisbon, Queluz came to represent the finesse and sophistication of aristocratic taste. Aloof from court politics and intrigue but possessing good taste and refined manners, as well as a considerable fortune, King Pedro was known as the *Capacidónio* ('capable and suitable', two epithets that he frequently used to describe people) and devoted his personal and constant attention to Queluz until the end of his life.

As Natália Correia Guedes remarks in her book, *O Palácio dos Senhores do Infantado* (The Palace of the Lords of the Infantado): 'the Palace of Infantes and

Kings, made a great impression on artistic society at the end of the 1700s; its constituent parts being drawn from various origins – the French, Germanic and Italian spirit that could be seen in it, wisely combined with elements that were already traditional in Portugal'.

Above: Aerial view of the Palace and the Upper Gardens.

Right: Façade of Ceremonies, overlooking the Hanging Garden, by the architect Jean-Baptiste Robillion, between 1764 and 1767.

MATEUS VICENTE DE OLIVEIRA, SUPERINTENDENT OF WORKS

Work started between 1746 and 1748. In a letter to the King, dated 8 December 1767, the palace steward, Agostinho José Gomes, commented: 'The royal residence of Queluz is twenty years of age, more or less the time when His Royal Highness created it; at which time it was handed over and was created little by little: the Architect, without any doubt, designed a massive building in just a few years'. Another

document, dated 1796, refers to 'the expense relating to desserts for the musician priests who went to Queluz to celebrate the feast of the Jubilee of the Works', and describes the start on the works as having taken place one year previously.

The individual mainly responsible for the building of Queluz and Superintendent of the Works was the architect Mateus Vicente de Oliveira (1706–1785), who also laid out, amongst other buildings, the Basílica da Estrela and the Church of Santo António da Sé in Lisbon. He was a student of the German architect and goldsmith João Frederico Ludwig (1673–1752), a naturalized Portuguese known also as Ludovice, with

whom Mateus worked on the building of the convent, church and palace at Mafra, completed in 1735, over a decade before the start of the works at Queluz.

Work proceeded well under the watchful eye of the Infante and increased in speed between 1750 and 1752, a fact explained no doubt by the great fire that took place during the night of 17 July 1751, reducing the Royal Court Palace in the capital of Lisbon to ruins. This was then being 'renewed in order to provide accommodation for His Most Serene Highness, the Infante Dom Pedro'.

Under the direction of Mateus Vicente, part of the Old Palace was demolished to make way for the construction of the wing known as the Central Body (*Corpo Central*), with a Façade of Ceremonies (*Fachada das Cerimónias*) on two floors, with a triangular pedi-ment, bounded by giant pilasters. Between 1764 and 1767 this façade was decorated by the architect Jean-Baptiste Robillion, with mouldings and masonry sculpted by Francisco António, mainly using floral motifs, garlands, cornucopias and shells. The vast windows, with their lintels also decorated with rococo motifs, are repeated on all the Palace façades.

As is the case with all the other state rooms, the Façade of Ceremonies faces inwards, unfolding around the Upper Gardens. By contrast with its very elaborate decoration, the outer façades are deceptively modest. This intimacy, only revealed after the outer doors are opened, induces a close and natural relationship with the elegant, French-style formal gardens, which were conceived from the very beginning as an extension of the Palace buildings.

Construction continued as far as the chapel wing, reaching the site of the future Music Room (*Sala de Música*) and the Throne Room (*Sala do Trono*). The façade overlooking the Malta Garden (*Jardim de Malta*) was later remodelled, sometime between 1768 and 1770. Its double pediment is broken and curving, contrasting with that of the older Façade of Ceremonies.

Lios, a type of limestone, common in the Lisbon region, was used predominantly throughout the Palace. It was strong enough to take decorative carving and came mostly from the quarries in Pero Pinheiro, about fifteen km from Queluz, where the stone was mined on a large scale. Other types of stone and marble were brought from Genoa.

Numerous Portuguese and French workmen were contracted. Timber was obtained from many places: much of it from Brazil, but some from Flanders, whilst planking was shipped from north Denmark and deal boards from Sweden. At the same time, the Chief Engineer of the Kingdom, Manuel da Maia (1677–1768), intensified work to collect water from springs in the surrounding hills, from 1754, building a reservoir in the Mirador and remodelling the aqueduct. From this tank, the water pressure was sufficient to supply the fountains in the gardens and irrigate the orchards, orange and olive groves, vegetable gardens and wheat fields both within the Quinta de Queluz and the neighbouring farmland.

Above: The main entrance with its iron gates. The plain outer façades contrast with those overlooking the gardens.

Opposite: The façade of the Throne and Music Rooms, overlooking the Malta Garden.

JEAN-BAPTISTE ROBILLION AND THE FRENCH TASTE

After the earthquake that destroyed Lisbon in 1755, most of the craftsmen at Queluz were summoned by the Marquis of Pombal to join in the enormous effort to rebuild the city. Mateus Vicente directed much of the building work in the capital, succeeding Eugénio dos Santos as architect of the Senate House of the Chamber of Lisbon in 1760. He was gradually replaced at Queluz by another architect, the Frenchman Jean-Baptiste Robillion (d. 1782), who left his mark on the Palace not only in his designs for the new areas undertaken at this time, but also in the decoration of many interiors.

His name appears in many different spellings – Robilhão, Rabalhão, Rubilau, Buillon and even

18

Monsieur Johon Bautistalon. Of his artistic career little is known other than that he had been a pupil and assistant to the great French goldsmith Thomas Germain. Germain was connected with Portugal on account of the richly worked royal tableware commissioned by King João V. Robillion had emigrated to Portugal in 1743 after he was declared bankrupt in Paris and his workshop closed down.

The first Portuguese document in which he is mentioned concerns a payment made in 1753. On 10 June 1756, by Royal Charter of King Pedro III, he was appointed goldsmith to the *Casa do Infantado* and charged with the task of executing 'all works in gold and all others as well as plans for those that may be ordered, not only for the Quinta de Queluz but any others that may be ordered for his use, benefiting from all honours, privileges and liberties that are enjoyed by other masters of crafts in his household, conferred by

the Most Serene House of Braganza'. A widower, earning an annual salary of four hundred thousand reals, he was granted permanent residence at Queluz, in the company of his sister, Marta. He remained there until his death in 1782.

A variety of talented Portuguese and French craftsmen assisted Robillion in modifying the original plan for the Palace, particularly in its decoration. Among them were Silvestre Faria Lobo, António Ângelo (woodworkers), Inácio de Oliveira Bernardes, João de Freitas Leitão, Bruno José do Vale, Giovanni Berardi (painters and scenographers), Jacques-Antoine Colin (sculptor), Guillaume Lautier (plasterer) and Jean-François Cragnier (cabinet-maker), to name but a few.

It was no longer a matter merely of extending the original manor house, the Old Palace. The marriage of Dom Pedro, announced in 1760, to his niece the Infanta Maria Francisca Isabel Josefa Antónia

19

Gertrudes Rita Joana of Bragança (1734–1816), seventeen years his junior and the daughter of King José and Dona Maria Ana Victória (future Queen of Portugal), made it necessary to provide Queluz with many grand halls befitting a royal residence. A Throne Room, not shown on the original plan, was begun at the end of the 1760s.

Robillion also added the west wing, containing the Ambassadors' Hall (*Sala dos Embaixadores*) and the private apartments known as the Robillion Pavilion (*Pavilhão Robillion*), housing the Don Quixote Room (*Quarto D. Quixote*), the Dressing Room (*Sala do Toucador*) and the Picnic Room (*Sala das Merendas*).

Although directly managed by Robillion, the works at Queluz were closely followed by the monarch himself. On 10 December 1759, he ordered the holding of a 'Stone Mass', which he attended together with the two architects and the workmen, as an act of thanksgiving 'for the columns and the stones having arrived intact'. It had taken five days to transport them, using 63 carts and 362 pairs of bullocks.

Corresponding to the King's bedroom, the façade of the Don Quixote Room includes imposing sculptures on the upper balustrade, representing suits of armour and allegories of the four seasons of the year, in the form of women and young men. Above the great central window, between the classical columns and capitals is a semi-circular arch, filled with a bas-relief devoted of Bacchus, attributed to the sculptor Filipe, about 1760.

Although neither the Ambassadors' Hall nor the Pavilion is described in the 1763 inventory (the oldest to survive), it is possible to place the start of their construction between 1758 and 1760, through records of

*Above: The Robillion Pavilion,
viewed from the Canal.*

*Opposite: The southern façade of
the Robillion Pavilion. The Don
Quixote Room is on the first floor.*

the importing and working of masonry, which continued until 1762. After that date, payments to craftsmen show that the decoration of the Hall was in full swing. The Pavilion was completed in the mid 1770s, forming perhaps the most homogeneous ensemble in the whole Palace in a successful marriage of architecture and interior decoration.

At the northern end of this wing, facing a tiled canal, Robillion devised the Lions' Staircase (*Escadaria dos Leões*) to overcome a difference in levels between the Hanging Garden (*Jardim Pênsil*), built above a large water reservoir, and the lower part of the gardens. The

Above: The Robillion Staircase, or Lions' Staircase, overlooking the Tiled Canal.

Opposite: Design of the Gardens, showing the Robillion Staircase in an earlier form, mid-18th century. It was changed on later plans. Watercolour drawing, 1080 x 1025 mm. (National Library of Rio de Janeiro)

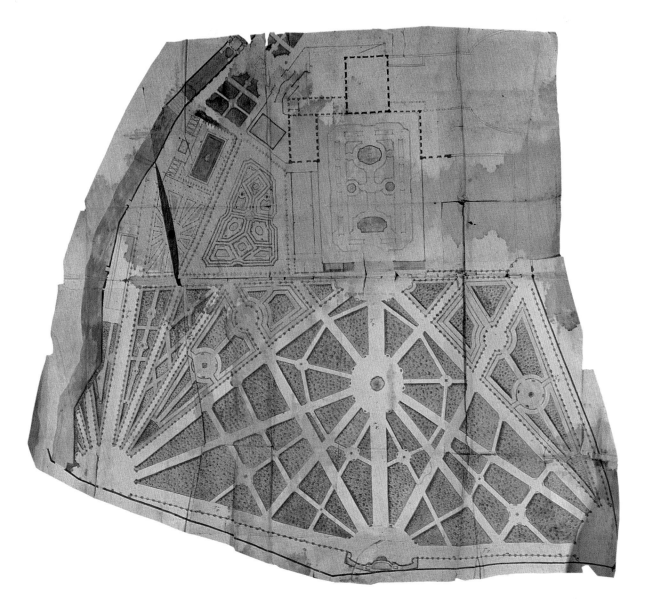

three sections of the diverging stairway, the balustrades and statuary on the terraces, combine with the location to create a dramatic and elegant effect.

On the oldest known plan, of before 1764, the positioning of the staircase is different. In an article for the magazine *Panorama* in 1855, the Marquis of Resende reported that: 'the Infante, already married to Princess Dona Maria, and King José I, who had a knowledge of the fine arts, were both displeased with the appearance and internal arrangement of the buildings within the estate (...) no less displeasing to them was the fact that the pavilion was not at the same level, and so João Baptiste Robillion was charged with remedying the offending feature.'

On 17 December 1778, the birthday of Queen Maria I, a new theatre at Queluz was inaugurated with the opera *Il Ritorno de Ulysse,* by David Perez, following performances at the Royal Theatres in Ajuda and Salvaterra. The Queluz theatre was situated at the south end of the Palace and was designed and decorated by the architect and painter Inácio de Oliveira Bernardes (1695–1781). He had already worked on the decoration of the former Opera House (*Casa da Ópera*), a portable marquee set up variously in the Music Room, the Throne Room or in the garden.

Also occasionally called the Opera House, the new theatre was built in timber, with boxes, a royal box and stalls, with decorations in papier mâché incorporating well known allegorical figures. For festivals, the interior was fitted out with damask and tapestries (from Arras in Flanders). The ceilings were decorated with allegorical paintings of musical themes. The theatre was dismantled in 1784, however, to make way for a new suite of apartments for the heir to the throne.

MANUEL CAETANO DE SOUSA, ARCHITECT

The architect Manuel Caetano de Sousa (1738–1802) was responsible for new projects following the death of Robillion in 1782. From 1785, he took over the supervision of work on the New Bedroom (*Quarto Novo*) of Prince Dom João, and a second floor that extended from the Ambassadors' Hall and the Façade of Ceremonies to the corner of the present-day Coffee Room (*Sala do Café*).

The new apartments, also known as the High Rooms (*Quartos Altos*), were for the use of Prince Dom João and Princess Carlota Joaquina of Bourbon, who had arrived from Spain that year and whose marriage to the Prince would take place in 1790. Work continued until 1789. Only the floor above the Façade of Ceremonies remains today, as the rest was severely damaged by a fire that broke out on the night of 4 October 1934, affecting particularly the Ambassadors' Hall and the Robillion Pavilion.

Manuel Caetano also assumed responsibility for the design of a new pavilion to house the apartments

Above: A postcard showing the first floor partly demolished after the fire in 1934. (National Palace of Queluz)

Opposite, above: An aerial photograph taken after the fire in 1934 shows the state of repair work. The damage is visible mainly on the upper floor of the Palace, in the area of the Ambassadors' Hall and the Robillion Pavilion. (DGEMN)

Opposite, below: The Dona Maria Pavilion, so called because she lived there as a widow. It is now the residence of foreign Heads of State during official visits to Portugal.

Opposite: The Dona Maria Room in the Dona Maria Pavilion,
now a drawing room for visiting Heads of State.
Detail: A tempera on canvas neo-classical ceiling panel in the
Pompeian Room in the Dona Maria Pavilion.

Above: One of the neo-classical
wall panels, in tempera on canvas,
in the Pompeian Room in the Dona
Maria Pavilion.

Detail: Tempera on canvas hunting scenes on the ceiling of the Hunting Room in the Dona Maria Pavilion.

Right: The Clock Tower, formerly accommodation for servants and storage, became a State-owned inn in 1995.

of the Prince of Brazil, Dom José. In order to position them at the southern end of the Palace, it was necessary to demolish the Theatre, or Opera House, as it was also known, only six years after it had been built. Amongst those working on the interior of the pavilion were the wood carver António Ângelo, the painter José António Narciso and the master decorator João Pedro Nunes. Documents relating to expenses for materials and fabric for covering the walls show that they were finished in 1789, one year after the death of the Prince of Brazil.

In that same year, at an already advanced stage of an illness that would lead to her madness, the Queen took over eleven rooms; the remainder were occupied by her ladies-in-waiting, stewards, her doctor and her personal confessor, the Chief Inquisitor, Father Inácio de São Caetano, Archbishop of Thessalonica.

Subject to modifications and changes of use down the years, since the 1950s this pavilion has been the residence of foreign Heads of State during official visits to Portugal. The presidential suite occupies what was once the Queen's bedroom. The building of this last wing completed the major works at the Palace.

A PERMANENT RESIDENCE

After the departure of the Queen and the declaration of Dom João as Prince Regent in 1792, the Regent continued the works at Queluz, which became the permanent residence of the Royal Family from 1794. There were some alterations to the interior, particularly in the construction of a service corridor behind the apartments, running through the entire building, from the Private Room (*Sala dos Particulares*) to the Chapel. This route is now interrupted by the frequent use of the space by the Museum departments.

In the grounds of the Palace, Dom João ordered the construction of buildings to the front of the property, facing the square, the most notable being the Clock Tower (*Torre do Relógio*) and, to its left, the barracks, both dating from the turn of the century. Designed by Manuel Caetano, the Tower followed a plan that he had drawn up in 1792 for the Tower of the Royal Chapel at Ajuda, which was completed by his son, the architect Francisco António de Sousa. The Tower at

Queluz was intended as a butler's pantry for the Royal Household, with accommodation for painters, sweepers, footmen and others and a clock with a dozen bells, installed by José Rodrigues Leitão. The bells were heard for the first time in July 1819, upon the news of the birth, in Rio de Janeiro, of Princess Maria da Glória; sixteen years later, she was Queen Maria II.

In 1830, a fire destroyed a large part of this complex, which partly explains the lack of character in its present interior. In 1995 it was turned into an hotel (a *pousada* or State-owned inn). This *palacete* and arcade, now Army Barracks, housed the Mews and Coach Houses of the Royal House and the Palace Guard Barracks, also providing accommodation for palace doctors, chaplains and servants.

Although not built on Royal instructions, the Palacete Pombal is also worthy of mention. This building, in the neo-classical style, is situated to the right of the Tower and was constructed on the orders of the 2nd Marquis of Pombal, Henrique José de Carvalho e Melo. It was intended to be his residence whilst staying in Queluz, carrying out his duties as a nobleman at the Court of Queen Maria I. It had still not been completed when the Royal Court was transferred to Brazil in 1807.

This not only put an end to the greatest period of activity on the Palace, but also prevented implementation of a scheme to enlarge the constructed area, as part of a larger intention to expand the town of Queluz itself. This is represented in a plan of the Palace and its surroundings, now in the National Library in Rio de Janeiro. It shows a major enlargement of the buildings at the front, with great attention paid to symmetry in relation to the rest of the Palace. It was projected to close off the entire courtyard, with an arcade and railings at the north and south ends. The plan was drawn up prior to 1795, as in it can be seen a pencilled outline of the short-lived architecture along the Chapel façade and the interior layout, as built during that same year for the baptism of the Prince of Beira, Dom António. It was probably made after 1789, as the Dona Maria pavilion was already drawn and the Tower does not feature on the plan.

At the end of the 1700s, the Prince Regent was responsible also for the construction of the road that linked the Palace of Ajuda to Queluz, for which he ordered leafy trees to be sent from as far away as London, and also for the opening of roads to Caxias, Sintra and Belas.

Elevated to the title 'Village of the Prince of Beira' in a Royal Charter issued from the Palace on 31 August

1802, Queluz continued to be the residence of Queen Carlota Joaquina until her death in 1830. Up to 1834, during the bloody period of the struggles, it was the temporary home of her two sons, Dom Miguel and Dom Pedro IV. Queen Maria II and her second husband, Dom Fernando de Saxe Coburg Gota preferred living at the Pena Palace (*Palácio da Pena*) above Sintra, where building work began in 1844 on the instructions of the King Consort, on the site of a former sixteenth-century Hieronymite convent. Dom Fernando removed some furniture from Queluz to the Palaces of Ajuda, Belém, Bemposta and Alfeite. But Dom Luís and Dona Maria Pia of Savoy spent the summer of 1874 at Queluz and it was also visited by Dom Carlos and Donna Amelia of Orléans, who carried out repair work. It was during this period that the Dona Amelia Mews (*Cavalariça D. Amélia*), commissioned in the French style at the turn of the century, was restored. The Palace was donated to the Portuguese State in 1908 by Dom Manuel II and, following his assassination, shortly before the establishment of the Republic, some restoration work was carried out.

Right: Palacete Pombal, commissioned by the 2nd Marquis of Pombal, in the early 19th century.

Below: Queen Maria Pia and her sons Dom Carlos and Dom Afonso walking down the Robillion Staircase. Attributed to Henrique Casanova, c. 1874. Watercolour, 350 x 550 mm. (National Palace of Ajuda)

The 1920s and 1930s again saw the need to restore the Palace and its interior, with a press campaign to raise the awareness of those responsible for the property. Through the General Board for National Buildings and Monuments, the systematic restoration of the interiors and gardens intensified around 1930, under the direction of José de Figueiredo, Raul Lino and Guilherme Rebelo de Andrade. The terrible fire that broke out in October 1934 delayed the works and it was decided subsequently not to rebuild the upper floor, which was less remarkable from a decorative point of view. The present pink outer plasterwork dates from that time, but the colour had probably been adopted only at the turn of the century; it is not seen in a watercolour of the Robillion Staircase painted during the last quarter of the nineteenth century. It had not been the original colour: remains of mortar and old plaster, blue-grey in colour and possibly marbled, were

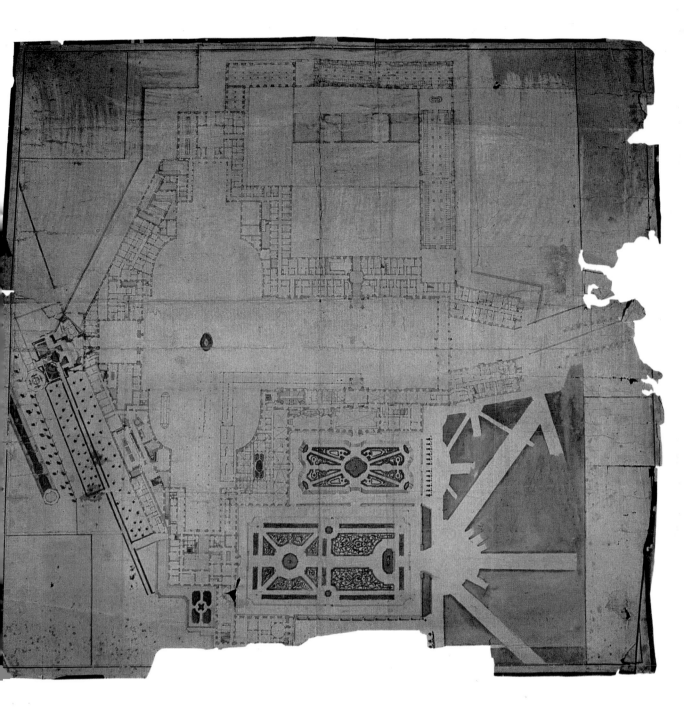

found recently on two different façades of the Palace, behind some marble busts that had been removed for restoration, and samples are now undergoing laboratory analysis.

The Palace was finally opened to the public during the 1940s, as the most representative monument of Court life during the second half of the eighteenth century, housing major collections of decorative art, some of which come from the Royal Household.

Above: A plan of the Palace and Gardens, before c. 1795, including an extension scheme that was not implemented. Watercolour drawing, 1140 x 1500 mm. (National Library of Rio de Janeiro)

Life at Queluz

History & Personalities

As a result of a disagreement that took place around 1760 between the Palace Steward Agostinho José Gomes and the French tapestry-maker Jean Malher, King Pedro III gave the order to proceed with an 'Inventory of all the movable property that his Most Serene Highness the Infante Dom Pedro had in his Royal Palace in Queluz, with the rooms numbered in order so as to have an understanding of what each contains'. This was completed in 1763 and is still the most valuable source for studying the Palace at the time of its original decoration, which has been subject to successive additions whenever major alterations occurred. None of the later inventories – dated 1767, 1776, 1798, 1807, 1851, 1908 and 1910 – has the same richness and documentary value, although they contain information about the numerous alterations to the rooms, particularly their furniture.

That first record described, from south to north, the outbuildings that were completed at that time, between the Room of the Halberdiers (*Sala dos Archeiros*) (Room 1) and the Music Room (Room 21),

together with much of their furniture and fittings, enabling us to envisage the levels of comfort and luxury in the Palace just a few years after its construction. In general, the walls were covered with damask, with velvet pelmets and carved door surrounds. Lighting was by means of a vast profusion of candelabra and chandeliers. The floors were covered in French carpets, running the length of the rooms, in brightly coloured floral patterns with contrasting borders, laid over rush matting which covered the floor tiles. In some less important rooms the walls were covered with fabric and original tapestries from the city of Arras, in Flanders, depicting biblical themes ('Sacred History', 'The Story of Moses', 'The Story of Judith', 'The Triumph of Joseph') and subjects from mythology (such as 'Diana in the Woods', 'The Story of Alexander', 'The Fable of Hercules with the Hydra' and 'The Story of Meleagro').

From an analysis of the documents that date from the first period in the life of King Pedro and Queen Maria I at Queluz there emerges an impression of great activity within the Palace and amazing versatility in the use of rooms, which were set up like stages and decorated according to the needs of different functions and events. The feast days of St John and St Peter were especially lively and were celebrated, as they are today, during the month of June, the latter being also King Pedro III's name-day. This was followed on 5 July by the King's Birthday. On 6 July 1758, the *Gazeta de Lisboa* reported that 'Their Most Faithful Majesties and Their Royal Highnesses celebrated St Peter's Day in the Country House in Queluz where the Most Serene Infante Dom Pedro entertained them with different types of firework, not only made in this city but ordered from Italy, and everything there was done with great magnificence, great profusion, good taste and good order.' In July 1760, the Court at Queluz also

Opposite:
Queen Maria I and King Pedro III.
By an unknown painter,
2nd half of the 18th century.
Oil on canvas,
2112 x 1750 mm.
(National Museum of Coaches)

witnessed 'several horse-races, a bullfight and, at night, a firework display and other amusements.'

Such celebrations often scaled the heights of extravagance. There are long lists of expenses relating to dinners and 'cooling beverages' for their Royal Highnesses and their guests, including dishes as diverse as cloves from Maranhão, cinnamon, pistachio nuts, cakes from Marvila, little savoury pies from Sesimbra, sweets from Odivelas, all types of game, a range of fish and seafood from Paço de Arcos. A single apricot dessert required '4,700 apricots, 105 kilos of sugar, 2 cooking pots and 22 dozen small dishes'. 'Cooling beverages' were usually served and for these were ordered plenty of ice for the sorbet and many sugar moulds, wine from Lafitte, in Bordeaux, Champagne, Burgundy, and 'cheeses from the Alentejo, both old and new'. In addition to the Royal Family and the Court, it was necessary to feed an assortment of priests, musicians and riding-masters, as well as an army of servants.

The painter and church decorator João Pedro Alexandrino Nunes was responsible for the design and mounting of the decorations in the Palace, as well as being charged with the redecoration of the bedrooms and Royal Apartments. These were all changed and cleaned in order to remove bedbugs – a commonly found parasite in those days – before new matting was laid, fumigation with lavender burned in perfume burners and the hanging of the rooms in light or heavy fabric, according to the season. The routine remained unchanged for decades and is recorded in numerous documents, although sadly there are no illustrations. Following the custom of itineracy that had persisted since medieval times, the Royal Family would leave the central palace at Ajuda to travel to one of the others — Mafra, Caxias, Alfeite, Salvaterra, Vila Viçosa. From the *Tesouro das Necessidades* (a kind of central furniture store) were sent – on these so-called 'day's journeys' –

furniture, tapestries, items of gold and tableware – to complement the contents of the different palaces – a fact which partly explains why the Royal Household's collections are so widespread today. The silver dinner service by Germain was often taken to Queluz under additional guard. When the Royal Family left, the carpets in each room – 'French carpets of all lengths and breadths' – as well as rush matting, were cleaned and rolled up until the next visit.

There were numerous kinds of entertainment at Queluz, especially during the years between 1752 and 1786, with music always playing a prominent part, even during the time of the Prince Regent. Before and after the building of the new Theatre, in 1778, dozens of musical evenings and operas were performed in the Palace. Musicians such as David Perez, Domenico Scarlatti, João Carvalho da Silva, João de Sousa Carvalho, António Leal Moreira, João Cordeiro da

Above: Wedding of the Infante Dom João (King João VI) to the Infanta Dona Carlota Joaquina de Bourbon. Inscribed, 'Souvenir des Fêtes celébrées (…) Epousailles des Altesses Serenissimes du Brésil en l'an 1786. Esquisse imaginée par Muzi'. Last quarter of the 18th century. Gouache on paper, 400 x 560 mm. (Maria do Céu Cupertino de Miranda)

Opposite: Infanta Dona Carlota Joaquina de Bourbon. Probably a copy of an original portrait by Mariano Maella (in the Prado Museum, Madrid), c. 1785. Oil on canvas, 665 x 555 mm. (National Palace of Queluz)

Silva, Luciano Xavier dos Santos and Marco Portugal all played their own works, including a large number of serenades inspired by themes from classical mythology. Happily, many libretti for these pieces have survived.

The birthdays of King Pedro were invariably celebrated in great pomp, as were those of Queen Maria I, the Princes Regent (Dom João's birthday coincided with the festival of Our Lady of the Conception, the patron saint of the Chapel, on 13 May), and the birthdays of the Prince of Beira and Princess Maria Francisca Benedita, when the custom of the Kissing of the Sovereign's Hand took place.

The celebration of religious festivals was compulsory, following a tradition that continued until the beginning of the nineteenth century, the important dates being the first eight days of Christmas, Twelfth Night, the first eight days of Easter and the feasts of São João (St John), São Carlos Borromeu (Carlo Borromeo) and Nossa Senhora do Bom Successo (Our Lady of the Happy Event).

Many foreign artists exhibited their work at the Palace, in the presence of the Royal Family and the Court. In August 1781, the 'young musician Francisco Farinelli', a castrato who was later to achieve great fame as a soprano, made his début here. One year later it was the turn of Pedro Delaval to go to Queluz 'with a form that speaks in the air, suspended by ribbons'; and Giuseppe Castagna, Director of the Compagnia de Fantocini, presented his puppet show. In October 1784, Francesco Gottlieb played 'the harp, beakers and tymbals'; in November 1794, Pedro António Favri 'cast a balloon into the air in the presence of His Majesty'.

At the end of the summer festivals, the revellers walked around the gardens, which were decorated and lit for the occasion, to the accompaniment of a firework display. In 1774, the painters, João de Freitas Leitão, António Berardi and Manuel do Nascimento, 'painted dummies set up in the gardens for the fireworks'. In his essential and pioneering work on the Palace, Caldeira Pires gives an account of the preparations in 1780 for the illuminations to be executed by Bernardo Foît for the decoration of the façades and gardens: 'great archways adorned with flowers and letters and other fantasies for the facade of the palace, the gardens, lakes and waterfall'. For the fireworks, 'the pyrotechnist Manuel de Sousa made 150 dozen illuminations, 14 dozen stars, 8 dozen vases of flowers, 10 containers of sparklers, 100 flying diamonds, 12 dozen pistols, 60 dozen mortars and 200 flying bombs'. To complete the picture, for the lighting of the garden,

'Francisco da Costa Carvalho made 98 large lanterns, 128 small lanterns and 130 round lamps'.

Life at Queluz and Court was still lively when the fiancée of the Infante Dom João VI arrived in Portugal. This was the first 'exchanging of the Princesses' between Portugal and Spain, and took place in May 1785 at Vila Viçosa. Sent at the tender age of ten to marry the Infante Dom João, the Infanta Dona Carlota Joaquina of Bourbon was the daughter of the capricious Queen Maria Luisa of Parma and King Carlos IV. Simultaneously, the marriage took place between the Portuguese Infanta, Dona Mariana Vitória, and the Spanish Infante, Don Gabriel. 'We sent them a fish and in return they sent us a sardine', said the people, slighted to have received a swarthy little princess in exchange for a grown woman.

The fortunes of the two princesses turned out very differently: the Spanish one was destined to bear nine children, suffer a life of conflict and to make a voyage across the Atlantic; the Portuguese Infanta and her young husband were both to die a few years later in Madrid; but their son, the Infante Don Pedro Carlos, to

Above: Horse-drawn touring carriage, in wood with gilt carving, lined in red velvet, with the arms of Queen Maria I. Portugal, last quarter of the 18th century.
3550 x 1600 x 1450 mm.
(National Museum of Coaches)
Opposite: Dom José, Prince of Brazil. By Miguel António do Amaral, signed and dated 1774. Oil on canvas,
1140 x 910 mm.
(National Palace of Queluz)

whom King João VI took an instant liking, was brought up in the Portuguese Court. There he always enjoyed privileged treatment, as may be supposed by the extension of the private apartments on the ground floor at Queluz, which were given to him at the end of the century. In 1810, in Rio de Janeiro, he was to marry his first cousin, Dona Maria Teresa, eldest daughter of King João VI. She would be left a widow just two years later, with a son, the Infante Sebastião. And so it

is that history sometimes repeats itself ...

At the Portuguese Court, the young Infanta Carlota had lived a care-free and happy life, according to letters that her nurse, Dona Ana Miquelina, wrote to the Queen of Spain, mother of the Princess, complaining that 'she never stayed still'. The Infanta formed what was almost a mother-daughter relationship with Queen Maria I, despite the formality of the protocol. She often behaved like a spoilt child, refusing to get up early or wear a corset – the bones of which snapped on more than one occasion – dilly-dallying over her breakfast chocolate and ill-treating servant girls and African women. In return, the Queen threatened to stop one of her favourite pastimes, rides through the gardens of Queluz in a cart and riding on a donkey's back. The lengthy obligations demanded by protocol and the never-ending 'Te Deums' must have been difficult for this eleven-year-old girl to bear, exiled in a court without other children and shortly to be overshadowed by a succession of tragic events.

Opposite: Dona Maria I. Attributed to Giuseppe Troni, probably a copy of the portrait painted from life by Thomas Hickey in 1783, last quarter of the 18th century. Oil on canvas, 1220 x 940 mm. (National Palace of Queluz)

Above: 'View of the Machine in the Garden for the fireworks, set up in the Real Praça do Commercio in Lisbon, on the happy occasion of the birth of his Royal Highness to the Most Serene Lady Dona Maria Teresa Princess of Beira. 1793.' Engraving, from a drawing by António Fernandes Ruiz. 590 x 510 mm. (National Palace of Queluz)

The death of King Pedro III in 1786 was followed two years later by the brutal and premature death of the heir to the throne, Prince José, who fell victim to smallpox at the age of twenty-seven. He left behind a widowed aunt and an already weakened mother, for whom the death in that same year of her personal confessor, Father Inácio de São Caetano, was another heavy blow. The political situation in France, where the French Revolution had broken out, greatly contributed to the Queen's loss of spirits. In 1792 she was declared unfit to govern, despite the efforts of doctors and consultations with the famous Dr Willis, physician to the King of England, George III.

In Prince José – the young visionary who had engaged the English collector William Beckford on his fleeting visit to Sintra – the Marquis of Pombal, an authoritarian minister whose service dated back to the reign of King José I, invested all hopes for the continuance of his work, even seeking the abdication of the monarch in favour of her grandson. For the use of José and his mother, building work had begun in 1784 under Manuel Caetano de Sousa on the north wing of the Palace – the present-day Dona Maria Pavilion. Queen Maria I came to live in this pavilion, giving it her name.

A PERMANENT COURT RESIDENCE

Because of the Queen's incapacity, Dom João was declared Prince Regent in 1792 and his first child was born during the following year. The birth of the Infanta Dona Maria Teresa was celebrated in grand style with decorations and fireworks, as described in great detail in the *Gazeta de Lisboa* of 31 August 1793. After spending the day watching jousting and bull-fighting, the festivities continued well after dark: 'At night came processions through the estate lit with Chinese lanterns, and the Palace façade that overlooks the gardens, with

Dom António, Prince of Beira,
a posthumous portrait by an unknown painter,
1st quarter of the 19th century.
Oil on canvas,
640 x 580 mm.
(National Palace of Queluz)

Opposite: Plan of the decorations in the Palace of Queluz, on
the occasion of the baptism of Dom António, inserted in the
manuscript 'Account of the Solemn Baptism of the Most Serene
Lord Dom António Prince of Beira. Celebrated in the Royal
Palace of Queluz. on 4 April in the year 1795'.
(National Library of Rio de Janeiro)

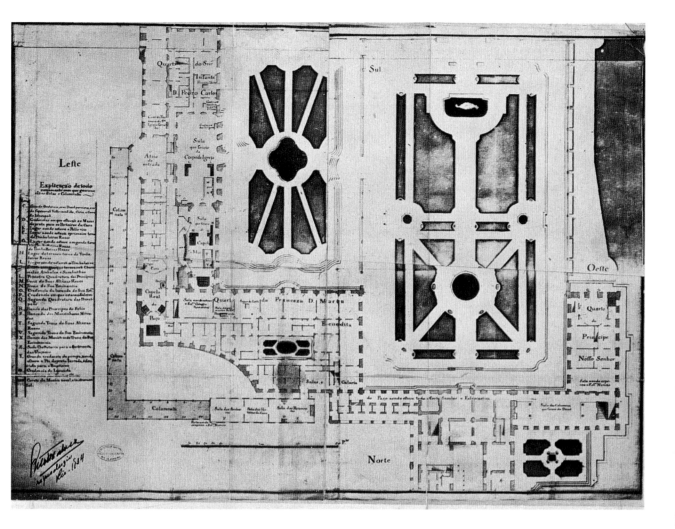

glass of various colours and transparent pictures, that by the variety of imaginary emblems, and the clever aiming of the lights, provided a spectacle that was both gorgeous and delicate. At the borders of the gardens were various transparent machines that moved around, showing the light of each one in a different perspective: at the entrance were two artificial water-falls (…) in front of the gardens was a waterfall that had been covered in transparent pictures representing the sea gods and goddesses, decorated with many lights (…) Among the trees, by the river, a great number of lanterns were set in a row, and on the river was a magnificent Chinese palace (…) In this place an Orchestra of excellent Music could be heard, and from other parts of the estate sounded the Music from har-monious wind instruments. Their Highnesses, the Prince and the Princess came out to see the illumina-tions, moving among the people who were there (…) They came to the new garden, where a balloon or air

machine was being made ready and being filled before setting off illuminated, and brightly decorated with transparent pictures, rising up easily until becoming lost to sight.'

Following the destruction of the Ribeira Palace in the great Lisbon earthquake of 1755, the nearby Alto da Ajuda was chosen for the establishment of a 'tem-porary' palace, as this was one of the areas that had been least affected. In the event, the Ajuda Palace accommodated the Portuguese Royal Family for almost forty years. Then, in 1794, after a fire at the *Barraca Real* at Ajuda, the Royal Family took up official resi-dence in Queluz, where the floor above the Façade of Ceremonies was completed in 1790 for the specific purpose of housing the large Royal Family.

Of the nine children born to Dom João and Dona Carlota Joaquina, only one, the heir to the throne, Prince António Pio, died without attaining his majori-ty, another victim of smallpox, at the age of six. The

Opposite:
Dom João VI,
the Prince Regent,
reviewing the troops at
Azambuja. By Domingos
António Sequeira, signed
and dated 1803. Oil on
canvas, 1000 x 810 mm.
(National Palace of Queluz)

Right: Dona Carlota Joaquina.
1st quarter of the 19th century.
Portrait miniature on ivory,
48 x 38 mm.
(National Palace of Queluz)

baptism of this Infante at Queluz took place in great splendour. Manuel Caetano de Sousa masterminded the building of the set-piece decorations that adorned the sides of the exterior façades facing the square and which the *Gazeta de Lisboa* of 11 April 1795 described as follows: 'The Chapel (…) not having sufficient capacity for that large function, led Our Lord the Prince to take the decision to hold the event in the Music Room, which was immediately made ready for the purpose with the greatest magnificence, setting up the Altar there. In order that the procession should come out of the Palace, a covered way was constructed, between the columns of which hung medallions inscribed with holy sayings from the Scriptures relating to the Sacrament of Baptism: all the aforesaid way was decorated with silk and fabric and the entrances from the Square were decorated with curtains.'

THE FRENCH OCCUPATION

Faithful to the old alliance with England and fearful of losing Brazil, Dom João VI refused to join the Continental Blockade decreed by Napoleon. On 24 November 1807 word came that the French, led by General Jean-Andoche Junot (1771 – 1813), were already in Abrantes and marching towards Lisbon. At that time the Royal Family was staying at the Palace of Mafra, from which they hurriedly made their way to Queluz. The last State Council met on 27 November 1807 and the Court then went into exile in Brazil, accompanied by large numbers of the nobility. They embarked from the Belém Quay on a sad and stormy day, as described by the Marquis of Fronteira in the

first volume of his memoirs: 'the Court luggage, exposed to the elements and almost abandoned, stretched from Rua da Junqueira almost to the Quay itself, and the carriages could not enter the square at Belém because the Prince's State, the immense throng who were in the square, the luggage and the regiment of Alcantara (…) impeded the traffic (…) A salvo fired by the squadron told us that His Royal Highness had gone aboard. Most of the families had become separated as a result of the confusion reigning, boarding the first vessel they came upon: most of the luggage remained on land, and much of what was loaded went in vessels separate from those of its owners, resulting in great privations being suffered by the Court during its long voyage to Brazil.'

The embarkation had been planned months previously and the ship the *Dom João VI* had been prepared for the purpose. From the 'Report of all that departed from the Royal Palace of Queluz for the *Tesouro das Necessidades* [furniture store] in February 1809' – in which the valuable contents of the seventy-four packing cases were described and in which it was noted that the majority were sent on separate ships, representing just a proportion of the valuables that followed in many subsequent shipments – we gain an idea of the magnitude of that terrible move. Much documentation of fundamental importance to a study of the Palace was either lost for ever or never came back, as was the case with the only two eighteenth-century plans of the Palace and its grounds – fortunately still kept in the National Library in Rio de Janeiro.

The period which followed was marked by three successive invasions by the French, under the command of Generals Junot, Soult and Masséna, between 1807 and 1811. The first was disastrous for the Palace of Queluz, as its new occupiers removed many pieces of furniture and silver items to adorn other palaces that they were using for accommodation in Lisbon.

Queluz was entrusted to the faithful steward João Crisóstomo, who never once betrayed the confidence placed in him by the Board of the Infante's Estate. In December 1807, Junot visited the Palace accompanied by several officials from the State Governing Body and the Board of the Infante's Estate, having given orders that he should be sent the ledgers recording revenue from the Estates and all the property belonging to the Infante's Household, as well as the plans of the Palace, where he intended to carry out some alterations. This interest and prior knowledge is not surprising, as just two years previously, in 1805, he had visited the Court of João VI in his capacity as French Ambassador, accompanied by his wife Laura. He had been well-received apparently. Now, his brother-in-law, Monsieur Geouffre, as he was known, ordered the Palace to be closed and he kept the keys. During the first and longest period of French occupation, lasting less than

47

IOANNI
PIO. LIBERALI. AVGVSTO
PATRI. PATRIÆ
MAXIMO. HVIVS. ÆVI. ORNAMENTO
REGIBVS. OMNIBVS. TANQVAM. EXEMPLAR
DEO. FAVENTE. CONSTITVTO
IN. QVO. NON. LVSITANIÆ. MODO
SED. EXTERARVM. GENTIVM
DIFFICILLIMIS. HISCE. TEMPORIBVS
SPES. POSITA
POPVLVS. LVSITANVS
IN. DESIDERII. GRATIQVE. ANIMI
TESTIMONIVM
HOC. MONVMENTVM
C

A. D. M.DCCCX

a year, Junot sought to realize his dream of installing Napoleon at Queluz. With this intention, he ordered the opening of the sky-light in the Lantern Room (*Sala do Lanternim*), known until then as the Dark Room (*Sala Escura*), commissioning the painter Manuel da Costa to execute a series of allegorical paintings to decorate the ceilings, a work that never in fact took place. In August 1808, the French were obliged to surrender, signing the Sintra Agreement which permitted them to keep their booty. Another of Junot's actions was the clearing from the Palace square of numerous dwellings and timber shacks belonging to Palace servants and functionaries, to enhance the dignity of the place.

On more than one occasion during the troubled times of the Peninsular Wars, the courtyard, the gardens and the Estate housed French or English soldiers, who were billeted there either in tents or inside the buildings, leaving a trail of devastation in their wake. As reported by António Caldeira Pires, 'On the morning of 27 March [1808] a new detachment of infantry arrived consisting of 327 officers and men with their commanding officer occupying the Board of the Infant's Estate, seeking in the name of the French Emperor, victuals and oil for lamps and forage for the horses. The soldiers were lodged in the barracks and the officers billeted in the palace, with the commander staying in the former apartments of Prince João and the other officers in part of the New palace [the high rooms overlooking the Hanging Garden] where 38 beds had been set up.' Following the routing of the French, the situation would be repeated, with the arrival of the victorious English troops under the command of Wellington, who had come to the aid of the Portuguese.

THE ROYAL FAMILY RETURNS FROM BRAZIL

The Royal Family stayed in Rio de Janeiro for fourteen years. They took with them the child who would lead this immense, rich territory to independence, the heir

to the throne, the Infante Dom Pedro. He was nine years old when he arrived in Brazil, but returned twenty-seven years later to Queluz, where his troubled life would end prematurely.

Unlike Queen Carlota Joaquina, who is reputed to have shaken out her shoes on leaving to ensure that not one grain of Brazilian soil remained, King João VI had not been averse to remaining in Brazil. Meanwhile, in Portugal, however, the swearing in of a new constitution had become urgent as a result of the 1820 Revolution. Before returning, the king ordered the carrying out of improvements at Queluz, to which he and the Royal Family proceeded a few days after disembarking in the River Tagus on 4 July 1821.

Queen Carlota Joaquina's conspiracies and her refusal to swear to abide by the new liberal constitution, taking instead the absolutist side of her son the Infante Dom Miguel, led to her banishment and exile in the Quinta do Ramalhão in Sintra, and also in Queluz. She was accompanied by the Infantas Dona Mariana and Dona Maria Francisca Benedita, ancient relics from the past, both of whom had crossed the

Atlantic twice; their sister, Queen Maria I had ended her days in Rio de Janeiro (1816). The obstinate character of Queen Carlota Joaquina caused her to be regarded with permanent suspicion by the monarch, who kept his wife under constant surveillance. Interesting accounts by the secret agents who monitored the Queen's contacts and activities were published in 1835 in a small pamphlet entitled 'The Secret Police in the Last Years of the Reign of King João VI'.

Separated from his wife, King João VI took up residence in the Palace of Bemposta, where he died in 1826, far from his two sons: the rebellious Dom Pedro, champion and leader of an independent Brazil, which had been proclaimed on 7 September 1822, but acknowledged only in 1825; and the younger son, Dom Miguel, who was exiled to Vienna, Austria, following a second absolutist coup by the Abrilada movement in 1824.

The King's death led to a succession crisis, which involved Portugal in a terrible and prolonged war between the two brothers, lasting until 1834.

Interiors

Principal Rooms

THRONE ROOM

The Throne Room, also known as the Great Room, is the largest of the three state rooms in the Palace. Its construction began in 1768, when the marriage of Dom Pedro to the future Queen Maria I required the creation of a large area for official audiences.

In the initial plan, by the architect Mateus Vicente de Oliveira, there were five rooms on this site, which are described in the palace inventory of 1763 (a note in the margin, of around 1774, explains that they were demolished to create a single room 'the size of which is as seen today and is the most beautiful and grand room to be found in Queluz'). A series of payments for work refers to the 'improvement to the Great Room' from 1769 and relates mainly to the masonry. In August 1770, a payment was made for large stones for the 'new façade', the present façade overlooking the Malta Garden. A document dated 1774 records the installation of window panes in this room, supplied by the warehouse belonging to Guilherme and João Stephens, from which it may be inferred that the room was in the final stages of completion, although it is not described in any subsequent inventory.

Designed by the second great architect to work on Queluz, the Frenchman Jean-Baptiste Robillion, the new room was in the rococo style, with carvings by the sculptor and wood-carver Silvestre de Faria Lobo. He

Opposite: View towards the altar in the Chapel. Designed by Mateus Vicente de Oliveira and decorated in the rococo style, this building was finished in 1752.

Following pages: A general view of the Throne Room.

managed a team that included Manuel José Sequeira, Crispim Luís de Mendonça, João António and Francisco António de Araújo. In relief on the white ceiling were delicate mouldings and gilded motifs, with fillets and tendrils in the French rococo style. The mirrored doors and pilasters reflected, by day, the light coming in through the doors and, at night, the brightness of many lamps, helping to create a magical atmosphere. The paintings on the ceilings representing Faith, the Sun and Hope (southern end), War, Justice and Charity (northern end) were executed under the direction of the painter João de Freitas Leitão, assisted by Manuel Costa, António Berardi and Manuel do Nascimento.

With French-windows overlooking the New Garden or the Malta Garden – originally a lake – the Throne Room leads eastwards to a courtyard, where the great wrought-iron gates now form the present-day visitors' entrance. A door formerly led off this patio to the Unoccupied Room (*Sala Vaga*), a kind of antechamber for the adjoining Throne Room.

Used in its early days for Dom Pedro's great parties and receptions, this room became the Canopy or Throne Room only in time. Immediately following the reign of Queen Maria I (1777–1816), the theatre was sited here, together with the apparatus required for that purpose. In the time of Dom Miguel, various plays were performed, including a famous one in which the Infante himself – later to be King – appeared in the role of Don Quixote, making his entrance singing an aria on horseback.

During the summer months, when the Portuguese Royal Family was in residence, official audiences were rarely held at the Palace, as the *Real Barraca* at Ajuda was more convenient for such purposes. The first recorded audience to be held in this room was that granted by Queen Maria I to the Papal Nuncio Vicente

Ranuzi in 1782. Although the Queen had been crowned in 1777, it was only in 1787, one year after the death of her husband and uncle, King Pedro III, that the first throne was fitted with the canopy or 'Dossel'. Designed by Silvestre Faria Lobo, this was on the wall opposite the Music Room and consisted of a golden carved baldachin, finished off with a shield bearing the Royal Arms, suspended between two dragons and ending in a large bow, from which hung yellow damask drapes edged in gold. The windows and doorways of the room were decorated with hangings in the same fabric, and the tiled floors were covered in rush matting on which French carpets were laid.

Down the years, the decoration underwent innumerable transformations, but these did not affect the furniture, apart from a succession of modifications to the canopy. In 1799, the Prince Regent ordered the replacement of the original, but retaining the shield and the figures. The master decorator João Pedro Alexandrino Nunes hung the new canopy with damask and silk in red, white and blue with a gold border, fringes, and gold and silver tassels. In 1806, the decoration changed to blue, and later on to crimson, in 1831. At the beginning of the twentieth century it was still possible to admire this carved gilt structure, in its original place at the southern end of the room, through which visitors now enter.

Between 1794 (the year of the fire at the Ajuda Palace, as already mentioned) and 1807, when the Royal Family departed hastily for Brazil, great Court receptions were held in the Throne Room.

In conjunction with the Music Room, this area was set up as the chapel for the baptism of all the children of King João VI and Queen Carlota Joaquina of Bourbon, with the exception of their first daughter, Dona Maria Teresa, who was born at Ajuda in 1793, and the youngest daughter, Dona Ana de Jesus Maria, who was born at Mafra in 1806. With the walls, floor and windows draped in black cloth, the Throne Room also served as a mourning chamber for Dom António Pio, King Pedro IV and their mother, Queen Carlota Joaquina.

In 1798 the layette of the heir to the throne, Prince António, was exhibited here, according to an anonymous manuscript kept in the National Library of Lisbon, written by a companion of the Papal Nuncio, who had travelled to Queluz for the ceremony of the bestowal of sashes, sent by the Pope. The manuscript states: 'We got down in the inner yard with the Iron Gate leading to the main House, where the Company of the Halberdier Guard was to be found with the two Ushers (...) and covering ourselves, we all four entered the Great Room, which was magnificently lit; in this manner we proceeded as far as the first antechamber of the bedroom of His Highness the Infante Dom Pedro Carlos, which was on the left-hand side (...); there we found four foot-stools for us to sit on (...) We went

*Above: The Throne Room in an
early twentieth-century photograph,
showing the carved and gilded
canopy at the southern end.
Right: Throne Room. Detail of the Atlantes.*

*Opposite, above: Throne Room.
Detail of the carving on the ceiling,
by the sculptor Silvestre Faria Lobo.
Opposite, below: View of the Throne Room,
with the doors open on to the Malta Garden.*

immediately to the Great Room, to which came all the ladies and gentlemen of the Royal Family with the entire Court to see the wedding clothes and gifts that were laid out on tables around all the room.'

These days, the Throne Room is often the setting for banquets held by the President of the Republic, the President of the Cabinet and the Minister of Foreign Affairs. A large number of musical concerts, put on by various important organisations, are also held in this marvellous space.

MUSIC ROOM

Designed by the architect Mateus Vicente de Oliveira, the Music Room was finished in 1759 and is therefore one of the oldest in the Palace. From the 1763 inventory it is clear that the structure has remained virtually unaltered down to the present, with '4 round wooden

columns imitating green stone' and the ceiling, 'round with an oval in the middle of half an orange', decorated with 'gentle carving with touches of gold'. The carved work on the ceiling, which is similar to that of the previous room, was again by Silvestre Faria Lobo and is in the same spirit, using musical motifs. The only architectural change to the room has been the addition of 'four windows in the eastern part, giving light to two inner courtyards', which were set in the opposite wall, overlooking the garden, and are now made into false doors.

According to the 1776 inventory, prepared during the lifetime of Dom Pedro III, this room was then fully furnished, with eight wall mirrors with gilt carving, 'eight chairs with rich tapestry, seats with rails decorated with figures from Aesop's Fables', and the floors covered in 'a red and white rush mat', on which an Aubusson carpet was placed stretching the entire length of the room: 'carpets from France in the same proportion as the house, surrounded by red and pink fronds (...) a pattern consisting of large tulips in red, pink and yellow (...) on a dark ground'. From the carved and gilt pelmets over the doors hung curtains of pearl silk, lined in yellow silk, with twisted silken cords and tassels. Set in an oval was a carved and gilt triangular canopy, hung with white and yellow silk fringed curtains. The room was particularly well lit, with eight wall lamps, carved and gilt with papier mâché around the mirrors – thirty-six candelabra, a large chandelier – 'a fine glass lamp sparkling on two levels with sixteen lights' – and four smaller chandeliers.

In 1793, the Moroccan princesses, women and concubines of Prince Molei Abdassalam, visited Queluz. At the end of the evening they were invited to admire the lighting in the Music and Throne Rooms, and Father João de Sousa, who was acting as their interpreter, described the scene: 'it being time to light the lamps they asked for the Glass Room, the Music Room and one in between to be lit and afterwards they were invited to see them (...) It was in no small measure that the princesses were filled with wonder at seeing the magnificence of those illuminated rooms, the appearance of which was so pleasing and brilliant.'

The Music Room, also known as the Musical Evening Room (*Sala das Serenatas*), was often set up as an Opera House, sometimes with the assistance of sailors, as in May 1770, when a group of 'mariners who came to draw the set of sails from the Opera House in the grounds of Queluz' were paid for their services. Until the inauguration of the new Theatre at Queluz in 1778, and again after its demolition, the Music Room was the setting for numerous musical soirées.

Because women were forbidden to appear on stage by decree of Queen Maria I, the female parts were played by castrati. A large number of musicians were contracted to serve the Queen and they were fetched in two-wheeled chaises whenever their presence was required. During rehearsals, 'cooling

beverages' were served, lemonade, maidenhair syrup, iced tea, coffee, chocolate, brandy and liqueurs, accompanied by cakes and biscuits. The golden age of music at Queluz came to an end in 1786, with the death of King Pedro III. The opening of the São Carlos Theatre in Lisbon, in 1793, attended by the Royal Family and the Court, contributed to its decline.

In 1799, the then Princess of Brazil, Dona Carlota Joaquina, chose the room for her Audiences and as her Hand-Kissing Room (*Sala de Audiências e Beija-Mão*), ordering it to be fitted with a new carved and gilt canopy in the oval part, which was erected at the same time as that in the Throne Room, under the supervision of Francisco Joaquim dos Santos.

In 1798, the Papal Nuncio was received in the Music Room by Princess Carlota Joaquina: 'The Audience was held in the great Room next to the Great Salon, which is the custom for audiences with that lady. This superb Room was magnificently illuminated; My Lady of grace [in state costume] superbly and richly dressed, accompanied by Her Most Royal daughter the Princess Maria Teresa (...) and Her Most Serene Highness, the widowed Princess Maria Benedita; the Lords and Ladies of the Court in state dress, the servants and officials of the Household with their uniforms and titles; which rendered it all a most worthy and dignified sight.'

Opposite, above:
Music Room.
Opposite, below: Music Room.
Detail of the ceiling.

Right: Music Room. Detail of the decoration, including representations of musical instruments.

PALACE CHAPEL

Also designed by Mateus Vicente de Oliveira, the Palace Chapel was one of the first parts of the building to be constructed and consisted of a single nave, and compartmentalized areas within the octagonal plan of the main chapel and choir. The dome of the main chapel was clad externally in copper and was in the bulbous German style, perhaps influenced by Frederico Ludovice, to whom Mateus Vicente de Oliveira had been pupil and assistant in Mafra, as mentioned previously.

The gilded carving was in the rococo style and executed under the supervision of Silvestre Faria Lobo – who worked at Queluz for thirty-five years, until 1787. It was completed in 1752 and consisted of railed panels, angels, garlands and volutes in gilded carving. The panels had mouldings with painted outlining and were filled with boughs, fillets and tendrils, elegant and perfectly executed. The carving at Queluz set a standard and had a considerable influence on the decoration of other religious buildings in the Lisbon area. As in many churches at that time, opulence was suggested at Queluz by the simulation of opulent materials in paint. The walls and ceilings were panelled in wood, with cloth laid over them, painted to simulate marble. The triumphal arch of the main chapel was flanked by two columns marbled to represent lapis lazuli.

Opposite: Detail of the inner cupola of the Chapel.

Right: Our Lady of the Conception, High Altar of the Chapel. By André Gonçalves, 1752. Oil on canvas, 2380 x 1450 mm. (National Palace of Queluz)

The retable of the main chapel, representing Our Lady of the Conception, the patron saint of Queluz, was designed by André Gonçalves (1687–1762) and completed in 1752. Other examples of his work included side altar panels representing St Francis of Paula, and the Imprisonment of St Peter and St Paul; the former was later replaced with a painting by Pedro Alexandrino de Carvalho (1730–1810). The paintings on the ceiling by José Gonçalves Soares also date from 1752. The 1763 inventory, which describes all the silver, hangings, missals and other objects, attributes the lesser-quality paintings near the high altar to the daughters of King José I: the *Saviour of the World*, to the Infanta Dona Maria Francisca Doroteia and *St Antony*, to the Infanta Dona Maria Francisca Benedita. The

image of Our Lady of the Conception on the high altar came from the Palace of Bemposta and was brought here by King João VI, whose birthday fell on this feast day, 13 May.

The organ in the choir, built by António Machado de Cerveira, brother of the sculptor Joaquim Machado de Castro, was brought into the Palace in 1778. This had also been at Bemposta and was decorated with carvings by António Ângelo, the previously mentioned designer of several carvings and models in gold, who in 1791 was appointed Master Carver to the Household and Estate of the Infante.

David Perez, Scarlatti and João Cordeiro da Silva all held sway over the carved and gilded choir during the Palace's golden era, when many Italian artists sang here, sometimes accompanied by members of the Royal Family. The chamber musicians of Queen Maria I were the subject of a eulogy by the English Ambassador, William Beckford, a connoisseur of such

Above, left: St Francis of Paula. *Side altar of the Chapel. By Pedro Alexandrino de Carvalho, last quarter of the 18th century. Oil on canvas, 2600 x 1400 mm. (National Palace of Queluz)*

Above, right: Imprisonment of St Peter and St Paul. *Side altar of the Chapel. By André Gonçalves, 3rd quarter of the 18th century. Oil on canvas, 2600 x 1400 mm. (National Palace of Queluz)*

Opposite: Exterior of the Chapel, showing the copper-covered cupola.

matters, who noted on one page of his diary, dated 26 August 1787, that the 'violinists and cellists in the service of Her Majesty are all first class and the flautists and oboists in her musical "ménagerie" are unrivalled.' In 1802, Marcos Portugal composed two psalms for the Royal Chapel at Queluz.

On the occasion of feast days, baptisms or other religious events, the chapel was richly hung with tapestries, damasks and silk, in colours appropriate to the time of the religious year. During Lent in 1765, the foot-washing ceremony that was normally held at the Ajuda Palace on either Maundy Thursday or Good Friday took place in the Chapel in the presence of King José and Queen Mariana Vitória, other members of the Royal Family and the Court. Many ordinary people came to see the 'Royal Family and the great number of rich and different coaches that collected together in the Square of the Palace of Queluz.' The event took place with great formality, according to a description by António Caldeira Pires: 'Dom Antão de Almada, having left his sword and hat in the Dark Room [nowadays the Lantern Room] and entering the Chapel, received from a Footman an engraved silver bowl which he placed under the feet of the first pauper, to the left side of the king and taking the jug, he handed it to the Infante Dom Manuel who poured the water with which the King Dom José washed the feet of the poor people. The Count of Redondo (...) received the towels from the hands of a Chamber Maid and as the King washed the feet of a pauper he gave the towel to the Infante Dom Pedro and he to the Monarch, and so they proceeded to the last pauper.'

On procession days, the exterior of the Chapel and various other façades of the Palace were also decorated with rich hangings, as in May 1784, on the occasion of the transporting of the image of Our Lady of the Cape

to the church at Cabo Espichel. In a carefully choreographed symbolic act, the reliquary of this venerated image formed the centrepiece of a long and curious procession, comprising many people and accompanied by eight carriages bearing 'Our Lady's silver'.

The Chapel has recently undergone extensive restoration, including cleaning, maintenance, a survey of repair work and reinstallation of the restored organ.

LANTERN ROOM

This Room leads to the Royal Chapel and, via a staircase, previously afforded access to the upper side platform of the high altar. From behind a screen, members of the Royal Family could attend services here without being seen.

It was known at one time as the Dark Room; the opening that can now be seen in the ceiling was created on the orders of General Junot during the time of the French Invasion, requiring the destruction of certain ceiling decorations on painted canvas. However, the decoration was never completed because the work was not paid for.

In December 1809, King João VI ordered that the ceiling should be restored to its original state. In photographs taken at the beginning of the twentieth century, it is still possible to see the exterior lantern, however, now destroyed, that gave this room its name.

The Regent, Dona Isabel Maria, trustee of the *Casa do Infantado* on behalf of her brother, the Infante Dom Miguel, also ordered the restoration of this room during his period of exile in Vienna, so that he could live here after his planned return in 1828. Although this never came about, a portrait of the Infante, painted in 1824 by Giovanni Ender in Vienna, still dominates the room and is the largest portrait in the Palace.

Opposite: Lantern Room.

*Above: Exterior of the Palace,
in an early photograph by Fillon,
showing the destroyed lantern.
(Library of Ajuda)*

*Right: Infante Dom Miguel,
in a portrait painted during his
exile in Vienna.
By Giovanni Ender,
signed and dated 1824.
Oil on canvas,
2056 x 1800 mm.
(National Palace of Queluz)*

APARTMENTS OF PRINCESS MARIA FRANCISCA BENEDITA

In the wing of private apartments adjacent to the Lantern Room, consisting of several small and intimate rooms, are the former apartments of Her Highness Maria Francisca Benedita, the youngest sister of Queen Maria I and widow of Prince Dom José, her nephew and the heir to the throne. He had been fourteen years younger and went to an early grave in 1788, struck by smallpox eleven years after their marriage.

She was known as the Widow Princess and accompanied the Royal Family to Brazil, returning with them again in 1821. She had lived there with her sister-in-law Queen Carlota Joaquina and came back with her to live at Queluz, pre-deceasing her by one year in 1829 and leaving no heirs.

are numbered from four to eight and they were then richly furnished, their walls lined with damask, with full-length carpets in vivid colours on the floors, central candelabra, carved door surrounds, pelmets in silk and velvet, and seats adorned with gilded carvings, as well as opulent chairs covered in tapestry.

Following the restoration work carried out in the time of King João VI, there are now indications of later

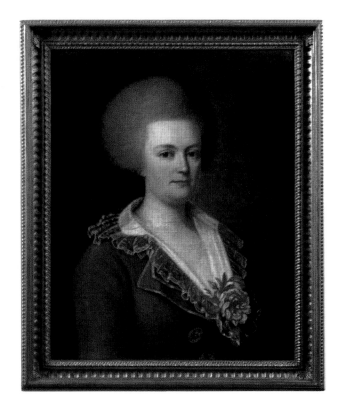

Above: Dom José, Prince of Brazil.
Attributed to Giuseppe Troni,
3rd quarter of the 18th century,
Oil on canvas, 623 x 515 mm.
(Centro de Apoio Social de Runa)

Left: Dona Maria Francisca Benedita,
Princess of Brazil.
Attributed to Giuseppe Troni,
3rd quarter of the 18th century,
Oil on canvas, 625 x 515 mm.
(Centro de Apoio Social de Runa)

Her name is associated with the Foundation for the Shelter of Invalids of Runa, set up in 1827 to provide a refuge for former members of the Portuguese Army, and a large part of the Princess's personal fortune was channelled into this charity.

In the much-quoted inventory of 1763, which describes the rooms from east to west, the apartments

Opposite: Boudoir of Princess
Maria Francisca Benedita.
The gilded and mirrored pilasters
existed formerly in other rooms in this wing,
coexisting here with more
recent neo-classical decoration.

*Left: Empire Room.
Apartments of Princess
Maria Francisca Benedita.*

*Below: Oratory in the
Apartments of Princess
Maria Francisca Benedita,
also known as the Chapel of
Our Lady of Carmen.
Altar by the wood-carver
António Ângelo.*

Opposite: Sculpture Room.

decoration in the neo-classical and French Empire styles, with ceilings and wainscoting bearing canvas painted in tempera. The Print Room of the National Museum of Ancient Art in Lisbon contains a series of six drawn plans for ceiling pictures at Queluz. These reveal decoration inspired by archaeological and Pompeian themes, palm trees, winged sphinxes, birds, garlands, medallions depicting sea ports in the style of Pillement, and motifs common to the French Directoire style. The value of the pictures lies not so much in their technique, as in the atmosphere that they would evoke in these rooms, which are on a more human scale than the others, creating a more intimate link with the gardens outside.

The first of these smaller rooms retains part of its original rocaille decoration, similar to that in the Music Room, with golden pilasters and mirrors across the corners. This may also be seen in other rooms in this

wing and it was described in the 1763 inventory: 'four corners of mirror glass inlaid in wood like the rest [of the rooms]', visible on the 1795 plan.

In the centre of this wing, in the direction of the Malta Garden, is an Oratory built in 1788. This is also known as the Chapel of Our Lady of Carmen, because of an image of Our Lady to which Queen Carlota Joaquina (who attended mass here daily) was especially devoted. After her return from Brazil, the image was transferred to the Robillion Pavilion, where the Queen's apartments were situated. Following her death, it was returned to its original position and has remained there ever since. The altar is the work of the wood-carver António Ângelo.

The three rooms that follow take their names from the functions they fulfilled in the second half of the nineteenth century, during the brief visits to the Palace of King Luís and Queen Maria Pia of Savoy. In the room bearing her name, the Queen installed her sculpture studio, whilst the next two were used respectively as the Smoking Room (*Sala de Fumo*) and the Coffee Room (*Sala de Café*), the latter being adjacent to the Dining Room (*Sala de Jantar*), which no longer forms part of the present-day apartments.

Opposite: Smoking Room.

Below: Coffee Room.

DINING ROOM

This room has been renamed, after the use to which it was put by the last monarchs. The notion of a dining room as an area is a relatively late one. Except for the Picnic Room – more intimate and situated in the heart of the King's private apartments in the Robillion Pavilion, with an allusive decorative theme – food was usually put on the table in different places according to the season, the personal taste of the monarchs and the location of their private apartments. And so it was that in spring 1779, Prince Camille de Rohan, nephew of the Grand Master of the Order of St John of Malta, who had come as an emissary to deliver Sacred Falcons to Dom Pedro, was invited to take part in a hunt on the Queluz Estate and had lunch in the forest. After visiting the Palace and touring the gardens in carriages, the retinue and guests were served lunch in the '*Barraca Rica*', probably the Ambassadors' Room which was sometimes given that name; the actual *Barraca Rica*, adjacent to the canal, not being large enough.

We should also mention the former existence of a room, now impossible to place with any degree of certainty, that was probably located originally behind the wing housing the apartments of Princess Maria Francisca Benedita. Briefly referred to in the 1763 inventory as 'Room No. 14', it was there that the table was laid for King José: '1 round table covering a tripod, covered in crimson with gold lace on which the King's table used to be laid. 1 ditto [table] covered in red gold damask with 3 leaves serving as a sideboard. 1 rich chair in red gold damask with gilt settings.' A custom prevailed at Queluz that attracted the attention of William Beckford who, on 30 May 1787, entered in his diary: 'This liking for putting skirts on commodes and tables is widespread here, at least in the royal apartments. In Queluz no gaming or dining table has escaped and I suspect that many old court clothes have been cut up in order to provide these adornments, which are in all colours, plain and with flowers, in country leaf patterns or splendidly embroidered.'

The present decoration of the Dining Room, with canvases painted in tempera in the neo-classical style, is no longer as it was described in 1763 under the heading 'Room No. 3'. At the beginning of the twentieth century there was a painting in the central panel – replaced in 1936 – depicting Hercules fighting a lion, supporting the theory that this room was also called the Hercules Room (*Sala de Hércules*).

The adjacent room, arranged like a museum to display the Palace collection of porcelain and ceramics, overlooks a small inner courtyard with a pool and is known by the curious name of the Otter Courtyard (*Páteo da Lontra*), perhaps because it was visited at some time by an animal of that name.

Opposite: Dining Room.

Right: The Otter Courtyard.

Below: The Dining Room, in a photograph of the early 20th century, showing a central ceiling canvas – Hercules Fighting a Lion – *that was replaced in 1936. (DGEMN)*

Following Pages:
Corridor of Sleeves.

CORRIDOR OF SLEEVES

This room is still called a corridor, despite being considerably widened during restoration work in the 1930s. It takes its name from the glass sleeves that were used formerly to protect candles from draughts, which it is supposed were kept here, in what was then a corridor connecting the old royal residence (or *palacete* of the Marquises of Castelo Rodrigo, as it was also known) and the new buildings.

The tiles of the upper part, of high technical quality and fine decorative effect, comprise neo-classical multi-coloured panels attributed to the ceramicist and painter Francisco Jorge da Costa, and date from 1784. They depict the Four Seasons, the Four Continents,

Right: Corridor of Sleeves, Spring.

Below: Corridor of Sleeves, chinoiserie decoration.

Corridor of Sleeves,
mythological scene.

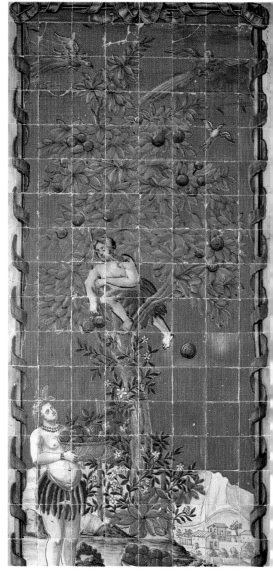

Corridor of the Sleeves,
details of its decoration:
America (above),
garden scene (left),
dancing dog (opposite).

scenes from classical mythology and, in the arch of the windows overlooking the garden, chinoiserie decoration. The older wainscoting is decorated with blue and white panels depicting hunting scenes, attributed to Manuel da Costa Rosado and completed in 1764. The room is furnished with blue and white vases from the Real Fábrica do Rato and with replicas made by the Fábrica Viúva Lamego, but also contains one of the garden carriages used by the Royal Family at Queluz, painted with Pompeian themes, and with delicately carved shafts and wheels. There are other fine examples in the National Coach Museum, Lisbon.

TORCH ROOM, KING JOSÉ'S BEDROOM AND OTHER ROOMS

The following four rooms, in the central part of the Façade of Ceremonies, are the most impersonal in the Palace. The place that they now occupy was identified in the 1763 inventory as 'Room No. 1 – Room which it is said was used for the guard.' The present-day names reflect former uses: the Torch Room, the Archers' Room and the Private Room.

The latter was where courtiers waited in the time of Dom João, when the apartments of the Prince Regent were on the floor above. Used in the time of Dom Carlos and Dom Luís as a Meeting Room (*Sala de Reuniões*) or Library, its walls were covered – even at the beginning of the twentieth century – with an unusual wallpaper. This has unfortunately been lost, but it may still be seen in a photograph taken at that time. Depicting battles between Greeks and Turks, it constituted a rare document, a late example of what is known to have been a common wall covering in various parts of the Palace.

In times past, the Billiards' Room (*Sala do Bilhar*) was situated behind, its walls lined with Flemish fabric. From here towards the Chapel ran originally the Chapel Corridor – but the course of this has been disrupted during successive work and as a result of new arrangements for the service areas.

This set of rooms is presently furnished in the three Portuguese styles that are most representative of Queluz – those of Dom José, Dona Maria and the French Empire. For instructional purposes these are arranged in chronological order.

Opposite page: Private Room.

Left: Dom José's room.

Below: An early photograph of the Private Room, showing the former wallpaper depicting battles between the Greeks and the Turks (from 'Monumentos de Portugal', Queluz, no. 10, Porto, 1930).

The Royal Family taking part
in a musical evening. Painting in
the centre of the ceiling, Ambassadors' Hall.
Copy of an original canvas
by Giovanni Berardi, 1762.

Top: Chinoiserie, coving in the
Ambassadors' Hall. Oil on canvas.

Opposite: Ambassadors' Hall.

AMBASSADORS' ROOM

Previously known variously as the *Barraca Rica*, the Room of Columns, the Musical Evening Room and the Gallery, after 1794 this came to be known as the Vases' Room or the Ambassadors' Room.

Work had begun on its construction in 1754 under the supervision of the architect Jean-Baptiste Robillion.

A 'small model to show His Highness the Infante' was painted in 1760. Although it was practically finished in 1762, it does not feature in the three earliest inventories of the Palace.

The French wood-carvers Jacques-Antoine Colin and Jean-François Cragnier both worked here. The painters Bruno José do Vale and Francisco de Melo were responsible for the paintings on the ceiling, on the mouldings of the cornices and on glass, representing allegorical and chinoiserie subjects. The painting on the central panel, scenically highly effective, is a

Above: The garden outside the Ambassadors' Hall: a lake set in trimmed box hedging. Opposite: The thrones at the west end of the Ambassadors' Hall.

replica of an original canvas, attributed to the Italian painter Giovanni Berardi, which was completed in 1762, but lost in the fire of 1934. Arranged around a balustrade against a clear sky, the Royal Family is shown taking part in a musical evening, presided over by King José I and Queen Mariana Vitória. Next to the King, playing a harpsichord, is the music master David Perez. The Infantas, daughters of King José, the future Queen Maria I and her sisters, the Infantas Dona Maria Francisca Benedita, Dona Mariana Josefa and Dona Maria Doroteia, all holding scores, appear to be singing. Conducting the concert is the King's brother, the husband of Dona Maria, the Infante Dom Pedro, crowned with laurel. At the sides of this composition are two other panels, executed in 1820 under the guidance of the painter André Monteiro da Cruz, representing Music and a Council of Gods on Olympus. In 1939, these panels were the subject of major restoration by the restorer and painter Fernando Mardel.

In 1767, the doors and windows were hung with blue damask curtains. Large Chinese porcelain vases, set on carved pedestals, completed the decoration, giving rise to the name the Vases' Room. Smaller vases, also oriental, were arranged in alcoves around the walls.

In the time of King Pedro III, concerts were frequently held here, in which the Infantas themselves sometimes played and sang, accompanied by their music masters, so that the room was also known as the Musical Evening Room.

The two throne canopies, bounded by mirror-work columns, were for the King and Queen, and the 'Princes of Brazil', so-called because they were the heirs to the throne.

Here, too, was set up the desserts table, which gave special emphasis to the last part of a meal, when the abundance of delicacies, sweets and fruit was matched by the exuberance of the table decoration, adorned with fine sets of china from Saxony, or with silver.

The oldest description is that by Giuseppe Gorani, who describes having found the Palace furnished 'with elegance and taste', calling it a 'place of leisure', and referring to this particular room as an 'Audience Salon,

paved with marble, the walls lined with mirrors and where there are seven great porcelain dinner services.'

In 1784, as the day approached for the arrival of the young Infanta Dona Carlota Joaquina of Bourbon, fiancée of the Infante Dom João, plans were made for the accommodation of the future couple. So, between 1785 and 1790, a first floor was built over the Ambassadors' Room, known as the New Room. This was destroyed in the great fire of 1934.

From 1794, when Queluz became the permanent residence of the Royal Family, until the departure for Brazil in 1807, the salon downstairs was used by the Prince Regent, Dom João for his kissing of hands ceremonies, and for audiences with the diplomatic corps and foreign ministers, who came to present their credentials. As a result, it became known as the Ambassadors' Room.

It was here in 1794 that the Prince received the English traveller, William Beckford, who was most anxious to be presented at Court. He reported: 'It was in the long state gallery, where the Prince usually received

Opposite and above: Chinese scenes of children. Details from the great Chinese porcelain vases in the Ambassadors' Hall, mid-19th century.

the compliments of the Court on birthdays and feast days – a majestic room, richly gilded and adorned with colossal porcelain vases, with vast profiles like Grenadier guards – that His Highness granted me an audience. He stood alone in that vast room, apparently absorbed in thought. He appeared to brighten with my arrival; although far from handsome, his unusual face had a wise expression which was at the same time singularly good-humoured (...)

"I hope you have had a pleasant journey?" His Royal Highness enquired.

"Considerably better than I had feared," I replied.'

In June 1798, the Papal Nuncio was also received here when he brought Holy Sashes from the Pope for the heir to the throne, Dom António, 'finding the salon very well lit and lined on all sides by the servants and officers of the Household with their fine uniforms and all their titles (...) a most magnificent and distinguished sight.'

In October of the same year, the Chapter of the Most Illustrious Order of the Golden Fleece was held in this room, at which the insignia of the Order was conferred by the Prince Regent on Luís Pinto de Sousa Coutinho, a State Adviser. The salon was hung with red damask and the other Knights of the Order were seated on stools lined with crimson velvet, according to rank.

In 1820, prior to the return of the Court from Brazil, repairs were carried out on the orders of King João VI. On 8 July, the Viscount of Vila Nova da Rainha, in a letter addressed to the Palace steward, João Crisóstomo, reported that the King 'is satisfied with the completion of the repairs to the Palace of Queluz and hopes that they will last out their time. His Majesty will await the bill for the costs as soon as the painting of the ceilings and decorations in the Vase Room are finished.' Several canvases were then scraped off and new pictures executed under the direction of the master André Monteiro da Cruz, who had come to Queluz to lead a team of around eighty painters.

The room appears to have been sparsely furnished, with only a few alterations through the years, primarily to the four chairs under the canopies, serving as thrones. It is here that the decorative effect of chinoiserie is best seen, a style very popular in the second half of the eighteenth century and well represented both by the profusion of vast Chinese vases and in the painting of the ogival coving. Some of the porcelain that was originally here was moved later to other palaces, as described by Dora Wordsworth in her diary (1847): 'The Vase Room is a majestic salon from which many of the oriental objects that formed part of its original decoration have been taken to [the Palace of] Belém.'

ROBILLION PAVILION

Immediately adjacent to the Ambassadors' Room, and currently known by the name of the French architect who designed and decorated it throughout, this wing has great decorative coherence and unity, despite the restoration work carried out early in the twentieth century, immediately before and after the fire of 1934.

Located in it are the private apartments of King Pedro III, King João VI, Queen Carlota Joaquina and, for shorter periods, Dom Miguel and King Pedro IV. It is the only part of the Palace to be floored in parquet tiles, made from exotic Brazilian timber, mainly holy wood and satinwood.

On the site of this pavilion, there had stood a riding-school, until it was demolished in 1784. This is revealed indirectly by a document on the 'demolition of walls and using the stones to make cobblestones (...)', which mentions the need 'to fortify the rooms above the riding-school, after the demolition of this had begun [the Don Quixote Room]'. In 1789, there is a reference to the arrangement of the 'houses that had been a riding-school for the accommodation of servants.' Striated flagstones are still in evidence today at the entrance to the ground floor of the Don Quixote Room, similar to those used in other equestrian areas, suggesting that this was once the entrance to the riding-school.

In the corridor next to the Don Quixote Room there used to be a staircase down to a cellar, which is marked on two plans of the Palace, one of before 1795 and another made early in the nineteenth century, showing the 'Former Apartments of Dom Miguel'. A further staircase existed between the 'Queen's Room' and the Picnic Room, so that these apartments were connected with this floor and the cellar, which was at that time inhabited. This access was not replaced after the serious fire of 1934.

Opposite: Queen's Dressing Room, Robillion Pavilion. Papier mâché in the rocaille style, with panels illustrating the various stages of male and female toilette.

DISPATCH ROOM

With neo-classical decorations covering the walls, this room contains oil paintings on canvas depicting ancient ruins by the Italian landscape artist Giovanni Berardi. According to Simonetta Luz Afonso and Ângela Delaforce, these were inspired by F. T. Charpentier's 1761 engravings of pictures by Giovanni Paolo Panini (1691–1765). A large ceiling panel represents an allegory of the *Passing of Time*, painted in 1790 by José António Narciso. It was replaced in 1940 by another of the painter Fernando Mardel.

During the time of King Pedro III, the room was used as a waiting room for courtiers, as well as being set up for banquets and late-night suppers during the summer festivals of St John and St Peter. Dom João used the room for ministerial meetings, audiences and dispatches, and had a canopy installed in it. Later, in 1830 and 1874 respectively, it was the bedroom of the kings Dom Miguel and Dom Luís.

ROOMS OF PRINCESS CARLOTA JOAQUINA

Retaining its rocaille decoration of gilded and multicoloured papier mâché, over mirrors and framing canvases painted with figures of children, the Princess's Dressing Room (boudoir) offers a fascinating visual survey of the male and female toilette in the eighteenth century. The various stages can be followed in the room's eleven panels.

The paintings on the mirrors and ceiling here and in the adjoining bedroom were attributed by António Caldeira Pires to the painter João Valentim, under the supervision of the Palace Drawing and Painting Master José Conrado Rosa. They would have been executed during restoration work in 1799 and 1800, commissioned by Princess Carlota Joaquina. Both these paintings and those in the Picnic Room, in a similar style, are worthy of careful study.

The ceiling has a floral decoration, within a suggestion of open basketwork, to a design that is echoed in the parquet flooring. The floral theme is repeated on the exterior of this room, where the central window balustrade of the façade is crowned with a basket of flowers and fruit in sculpted stone.

Above: Queen's Dressing Rroom.
Young man powdering his hair. Oil on canvas.
2nd half of the 18th century.

Below: Young lady trying on ornaments. Oil on
canvas. 2nd half of the 18th century.
Opposite: The Ladies-in-Waiting Room.

The Dressing Room is bounded to the east by an antechamber, the Ladies-in-Waiting Room, whose canvas-lined walls are painted with medallions in tempera, in the style of Pillement, of landscapes in grisaille. It was here that the Queen's ladies-in-waiting gathered to receive their orders.

To the south and adjacent to the Dressing Room is the Bedroom, the only room in the Palace to have silvered decorations in papier mâché. In July 1776 a payment was made of 'one thousand silver pieces for the bedroom', which retained its original decorations until the early twentieth century, as described by Caldeira Pires: 'lined with mirrors with paintings of sleeping angels and children, stretching and yawning, works by the same painter as the previous room.' The author goes on to say that the room had been used as a bedroom down the years, for King Pedro III, Prince João and Princess (later Queen) Carlota Joaquina, as well as being the dispatch room of Dom Miguel.

On display in the damask-lined oratory associated with this and the Don Quixote Room is a small reliquary, finely worked and gilt, attributed to the sculptor-carver António Ângelo.

In 1828 Queen Carlota Joaquina ordered a state portrait of Dom Miguel to be placed here, next to the image of our Lady of Carmen. In the 1934 fire, the paintings in this room were unfortunately either lost completely or damaged beyond repair; this was also the case with the room's original decoration in papier mâché.

Dispatch Room, Robillion Pavilion.

Right: Decorative panels in the
Dispatch Room. By Giovanni Berardi,
after engravings by F.-.T. Charpentier,
after paintings by Giovanni Paolo
Pannini, 3rd quarter of the 18th
century. Oil on canvas,
2903 x 2003 mm.
(National Palace of Queluz)

Oratory associated with the Don Quixote Room, with gilded reliquary attributed to the sculptor-carver António Ângelo. Opposite: Queen Carlota Joaquina's Room.

PICNIC ROOM

In plan this room is square and relatively small in area.
It was nearing the last stages of completion in 1767,
when the carpenter José da Silva 'secured the roses on
the ceiling of the Picnic Room', within a decorative
structure suggesting a honeycomb.

With gilded decoration in papier mâché framing a
set of four large figurative canvases, and six overdoors
depicting still-lives in the rocaille style, everything in
this room suggests the purpose for which it was created: a private dining room to accompany the royal
apartments.

The four large canvases, which were painted on an
easel and then attached to the walls, are striking
because they have remained almost untouched. They
represent hunting picnics and are rich in detail. Ladies
and gentlemen, seated informally on the ground and
surrounded by their weapons and dogs, are engaged in

Above: Picnic Room, Robillion Pavilion.
'Summer', Hunting Picnic. By an unknown
painter, 3rd quarter of the 18th century.

Opposite: Picnic Room (above) and 'Winter',
Hunting Picnic (below), in the same room. By
an unknown painter. Oil on canvas, 3rd quarter
of the 18th century.

Following pages: Don Quixote Room.

the pleasures of gastronomy and conversation. The set
of canvases forms an allegory of the Four Seasons of
the year, as suggested by the dress of the figures and
the varying state of the surrounding vegetation. This
enables us easily to identity the picture on the wall by
the Ladies-in-Waiting Room as Summer, and that on
the wall facing the garden as Winter.

DON QUIXOTE ROOM

Built between 1759 and 1774 to a plan prepared by Jean-Baptiste Robillion, this room is square, but gives the illusion of being circular: a series of eight columns cut the corners and support the ceiling dome, giving it the name of the Round Room (*Sala Redonda*).

The decoration comprises a set of mirrors and carved gilt decorations in the rocaille style, framing the eight paintings on the coving and nine over-doors, showing scenes from the life of the Cervantes' character, Don Quixote of La Mancha, attributed to the painter Manuel da Costa (1755–1820). The ceiling, a perfect illustration of the neo-classical spirit, is completed by a central canvas, an *Allegory of Music*, attributed to

José António Narciso (1731–1811), a great ceiling painter during the second half of the eighteenth century. This was retouched by Fernando Mardel in 1940, as were many of the paintings on the coving and over-doors. In 1771, the chequerboard floor was laid.

During the reign of Queen Maria I and King Pedro III the dessert table was set up here, adjoining the Ambassadors' Room, as corroborated by documentation relating to the year 1774, when two painters were engaged and a lady was paid to make 212 artificial flowers. The table was set with great opulence, displaying countless figures in silver and porcelain, mostly representing a great variety of mythological and exotic figures. The Palace Inventory of 1763 refers to a series of '25 dessert figures' in silver, including: five male figures representing heroism and five representing Jupiter, Pluto, Cyclops, Orpheus and Cupid; two boys riding phoenixes and two on seahorses; four female figures representing Venus, Minerva and Diana; another 'with a pitchfork with three teeth on the right hand which being a woman I have seen nothing like it'; and also two 'gold-perfumed' Indians with two cornucopias serving as candlesticks. In 1763 a rich dessert holder in Meissen porcelain came to the Palace from Castile. It is around two metres in length and one wide, standing on bronze feet and divided into twelve parts. A mirror-back reveals a miniature of a garden,

with dozens of mythological figures, hundreds of buildings, verandahs, balustrades, pots of flowers, springs and dolphins spouting water, box trees, rocks and sand, all in white porcelain picked out in green and gold. Surrounding this centrepiece are dozens of other pieces representing animals, hunters, the seasons of the year, different parts of the world, allegorical figures and different fruits, 'in colours so like their own that each could be mistaken for the natural one.'

On more important state occasions, when the Germain dinner service was brought to Queluz from the Ajuda Palace, the large number of precious items required an additional guard. During July 1774, payment was made 'to a man who for several nights guarded the Dessert Silver and the Silver Centre.' Various foreign travellers have made reference to this room. The first was Gorani (1767), who especially liked the 'paintings that depicted the story of Don Quixote.'

With the exception of the three larger rooms, this is the best known state room in the Palace, where Royal Personages were born and died. It was here that the children of King João VI and Queen Carlota Joaquina came into the world, including the Infante Dom Pedro, future Emperor of Brazil and then King Pedro IV of Portugal. In 1828, King Miguel convalesced here after fracturing his femur. The Prince of Lichnowsky, who visited in 1842, described 'a vast red

Morocco leather day bed where the ailing King João VI lay, where Dom Miguel (...) suffered and where Dom Pedro took his last breath. I dared to lie on it despite an awareness of my lowly status.'

The room has always been linked particularly to the memory of Pedro IV, the restorer of the Portuguese constitutional monarchy, who died of tuberculosis, aged just thirty-six. In 1850, his daughter Princess Maria Amelia, who was to succumb to the same illness the following year in Funchal, aged twenty-one, inspected the room and noted in French in the margin of a watecolour by the Ferdinand le Feubure: 'The room where my father died in the Palace of Queluz.' When Dora Wordsworth visited the Palace in 1847, she observed: 'the romantic emperor who fought for liberty, died in a room whose very name has a foreboding ring.' Something of a knight errant, the subject matter of the paintings was indeed appropriate to his nature.

Tradition has it that he expired on a canopied bed, attended by his second wife Dona Amelia de Leuchtenberg Beauharnais, his daughter Queen Maria II, who had been crowned just one week earlier (aged sixteen) and the ministers and generals who had helped him to victory during the liberal revolution. Just before he died, he bade a symbolic farewell to his army by embracing a soldier, depicted in a highly romantic engraving by N. Maurin and L. de Maurin.

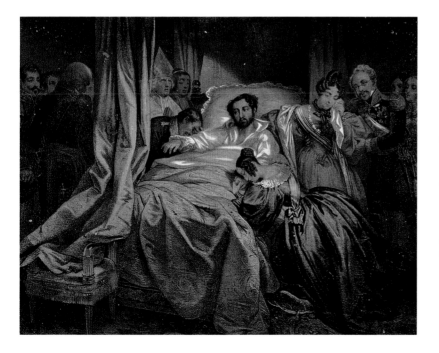

Opposite page, above: Don Quixote Room, overdoor, Don Quixote Tilting at Windmills. *Oil on canvas.*

Opposite page, below: Watercolour of the Don Quixote Room, by Ferdinand le Feubure, 1850. It has an inscription by Princess Maria Amelia, daughter of King Pedro IV: 'The room where my father died in the Palace of Queluz.'
201 x 320 mm.
(Gal. Biedermann, Munich)

Death of King Pedro IV.
Hand-coloured engraving, Paris, c.1834. 315 x 365 mm.
(National Palace of Queluz)

The Gardens

Leisurely Festivities

Perceived as a natural extension of the rooms of the Palace, whose façades open on to them, the magnificent gardens of Queluz have always been tended with great care. At its foundation, the Royal Estate of Queluz was formed around a collection of properties that had been acquired by King Pedro III. To these, King João VI added the New Estate, also known as the Great Property, the Quinta de Queluz de Baixo and the Quinta do Rebelo.

Today, however, the Estate has been reduced to its immediate surroundings and grounds, comprising an area of around fifteen hectares, divided into the upper gardens on the one hand and the park on the other. On the opposite side of the Lisbon—Sintra road, which borders the Palace to the south, is the *Matinha* (or 'Little Forest'), with its fine gateway flanked by pinnacles. The Little Forest was formerly connected to the main Palace Estate by a bridge.

UPPER GARDENS IN THE FRENCH STYLE

Designed by Robillion according to formal French geometric models, the two upper gardens, the Malta Garden and the Hanging Garden, are divided from each other and from the rest of the park by a balustrade. The lines of box trees in their pots give the idea of an embroidery, but one of limited size and circumscribed views, by comparison with the great French gardens of Versailles or Vaux-le-Vicomte, for example. This is because of the terrain of the gardens themselves, where no levelling of the ground took

Panoramic view of the Hanging Garden.

place. The view from the broad walk could not be extended, therefore, as far as the Great Waterfall (*Cascata Grande*). The gardens were adorned with lakes, urns and statues made of Italian marble, together with magnificent sculptural groups, cast in lead, from the London studio of the sculptor John Cheere.

The majority of the sculptures were added to the Palace gardens between 1755 and 1765. The marble statues were commissioned in Italy through the Italian Nicolau Possolo, who lived in Lisbon. In London, sculptures were commissioned through the bankers, Thomas & Thomas, and were probably chosen by the Portuguese Ambassador, Dom Luís da Cunha.

Some of the sculptural details, in the design of the formal ponds in particular, are reminiscent of delicate goldsmiths' work – possibly because Robillion had once been a pupil of the famous French goldsmith Thomas Germain.

The statuary that adorns around fifteen hectares of park and gardens is richly varied in its themes and

Above and opposite: Topiary box hedging in the Malta Garden.

subject matter, but it is difficult to discover any coherence of plan, a point made in a study by Simonetta Luz Afonso and Angela Delaforce. They were able to identify almost all the existing sculptures in contemporary inventories. Some of the figures have been moved around at various times; a few waited many years after their arrival before the right place was found for them, during which time their condition deteriorated.

Although there is no symbolism in the distribution of the sculptures, the criteria for which appear to have been purely decorative, the themes are taken predominantly from classical mythology, including such figures as Diana, Neptune, Ceres, Mercury, Bacchus, heroes and heroines, nymphs and satyrs. Watery themes are much in evidence in the decoration of the lakes and fountains – Neptune, Venus, tritons, sirens and fish. Various allegories of the Four Seasons of the year and the arts, figures from the Commedia dell'Arte, shepherds and animals complete this heterogeneous combination, which was very much to eighteenth-century taste.

MALTA GARDEN

The Malta Garden, facing the façades of the Throne and Music Rooms, takes its name from the Order of the Knights of St John of Malta, of which King Pedro III was Grand Master, a title held by all the Lords of the Household of the Infante's Estate. It was also known as the Laurel Cherry Garden, because it contained bushes of that species imported from the Netherlands in 1758. In that year alone, 1,450 laurel cherry bushes were brought across from Amsterdam.

The garden occupies the area where the so-called 'cypress tank' originally stood, which is recorded to have displayed in its centre a male figure holding up a cornucopia, from which he emptied water. The tank was demolished in 1758 and the stones from which it was built were used for the Robillion staircase. These days, there are four marble sculptures representing the arts – Music, Painting, Sculpture and Architecture – in the middle of this area, surrounding a pool with a central group of three boys frolicking with a dolphin. Until the early twentieth century, there were also small tanks in each of the four corners of the garden, with figures of boys pouring water, but these have been removed: two have been relocated amongst the fountains and the others in one of the circular intersections on the park's radial broad walks.

On either side of the exterior doorway to the Throne Room, two female figures in marble represent Ceres and Flora. At the eastern end, above the balustrade, there are six sculptural groups in white marble representing childhood scenes. These have been in that location since the elegant gardens were initially designed and laid out; their position is recorded in the 1763 inventory.

Above: Detail of the steps around the Malta Garden.

Left: A sculpted group in white marble, from the balustrade to the east of the Malta Garden. Italy, 3rd quarter of the 18th century.

Opposite: View of the Hanging Garden, from the first-floor window of the Façade of Ceremonies, with Neptune's Lake in the foreground and the Knight's Gate in the background.

HANGING GARDEN

This is called the Hanging Garden because it is built over a reservoir that collects water from upper garden lakes, in an architectural solution devised by Robillion to overcome differences in ground level and to raise this area to the height of the Façade of Ceremonies. It is also sometimes known as the New Garden or Neptune's Garden.

A document dating from 1758 states that a drainage system is to be constructed here. The purchase of 'string to mark out the garden', in 1765 is an indication that they were starting to plan the parterre of box trees; roots of box were ordered to be sent from

Belém (Lisbon), from the house of the Viscount of Ponte de Lima e de Ourém. However, the majority of trees – chestnut, elm, box and myrtle – as well as gardening implements, had come directly from the Netherlands at the start of construction work on the Palace and its gardens. In November 1754, a shipment of around five hundred trees and three hundred box pyramids left Amsterdam.

From 1755, the Dutch gardener, Van der Kolk took charge of planting with the assistance of the Palace gardener, Luís Simões Ressurgido.

In the centre of the Hanging Garden are two imposing lakes, both decorated with sculptural groups from the London studio of John and Henry Cheere. Neptune's Lake, near the Façade of Ceremonies, is surrounded by six lead sculptures representing the Four

Seasons and figures from mythology; the sculptures around the Lake of Venus, also known as the Lake of the Nereid, represent 'Thetis sitting on a dolphin, inside a Stone Shell in the form of a Gun-boat, borne by tritons, Tagus and Guadiana, Fountain Boys, tritons and dolphins.' At the ends of the garden's lesser axis are two smaller lateral ponds, with singeries in lead, popularly known as the 'monkey tanks'.

Many of the statues were originally painted in bright colours or partly gilded, as stated in a document dated 1789, which records that the painter António Narciso 'painted all the pyramids of the water-jets in gold and various colours with walnut oil' and cleaned them regularly.

A document dated 1826 transcribes the recipe for the solution that was used in the

Opposite: The west side of the Hanging Garden and, below, a detail of a stone sphinx.

Right: Neptune's Lake, incorporating a group of lead sculptures from the London studio of John Cheere, 3rd quarter of the 18th century. Below is a detail, of a lead serpent wrapped around a stone globe.

Following pages: The Lake of Venus or the Nereid, with lead sculptures from the studio of John Cheere, 3rd quarter of the 18th century.

monthly cleaning, stating the ingredients, proportions and methods to be used: 'Vitriolic Ether (3), Vitriolic Spirit (18) and Refined Saltpetre (6), applied with a sponge and brushes.'

The Hanging Garden appears to have been completely finished during the 1770s, because in 1772 the painter João Berardi executed an enormous fresco, which has since unfortunately disappeared, on the wall supporting it. This depicted the game of blindman's buff: 'a picture showing blindman's buff giving the appearance of a fresco, on the wall supporting the large garden, that faces the Labyrinth.'

KNIGHTS' GATE AND
GREAT WATERFALL

The Knights' Gate (*Pórtico dos Cavaleiros*), with a balustrade decorated with statues and urns, separates the Upper Gardens from the park and the agricultural area. It depicts *Heroic Fame Mounted on Pegasus*, by the sculptors Manuel Alves and Filipe da Costa. In 1771, 83 bullock carts and 180 men were needed to drag two great stones from Vila Chã for its construction, and two years later the stone horses were raised into position with the assistance of sailors. This gateway, from which the avenues radiate out into the park within a network of secondary paths interrupted by water, is flanked by two great water tanks. It marks the former main approach to the Palace, ending to the north at the Façade of Ceremonies, whose main door is guarded by two imposing lead sculptures by John Cheere, representing Mars and Minerva. To the south, lies the Great Waterfall.

Built during the 1770s, this waterfall appears on the early plan now kept in the Library in Rio de Janeiro. It was covered with pieces of worked stone and rock from Cascais. The water spouted from a channel of hewn stone, with a large reservoir above and a verandah decorated with lead and marble statues. As was common in many gardens of those times, the waterfall was the single most spectacular feature of the entire water garden and fountain system.

The water supply for all the lakes was the Miradouro tank, a reservoir beyond the Palace walls, into which flowed, via the Ponte Pedrinha Aqueduct, the water from the main springs in the region, but these have unfortunately disappeared with the urban growth in recent years. The water from the lakes in the Upper Gardens was then collected in turn in the vaulted cistern of the Hanging Garden.

Facing the wall that supported this was the Garden of the Labyrinth, of which the outline remains in the oldest surviving plan, dating from the mid-eighteenth century, now in the National Library in Rio de Janeiro. This reveals that the Labyrinth was adorned with five gilded garden tanks and multi-coloured sculptures.

Although the park and gardens of Queluz have changed a great deal, it is not difficult to reconstruct the scene described by William Beckford in his diary entry on 14 June 1794, in which he described games there between the Infanta Carlota Joaquina, then nineteen years old, and her nurses: 'cascades and fountains were in full play; a thousand sportif *jets d'eau* were sprinkling the rich masses of bay and citron, and drawing forth all their odours, as well-taught water is certain to do upon such occasions. Amongst the thickets, (...) the Infanta's the nymph-like attendants, all thinly clad after the example of the royal and nimble self, were glancing to and fro, (...) laughing and talking all the while with very musical silver-toned voices.

There, continued she, "down that avenue; if you like, when I clap my hands together, start; your friend Pedro and two of my donzelas shall run with you – take care you are not beaten."

(...) Although I had given them ten paces in advance, exerting myself in right earnest, I soon left them behind, and reached the goal – a marble statue.

"Muy bien, muy bien," said the Princess in her native Castilian when we returned to the margin of the velvet carpet on which she was still sitting reclined, and made our profound obesiances.

"I can see the Englishman can run – report has not deceived me." Now, she continued, "let me see whether he can dance a bolero; (...)"

TILED CANAL: WATER, MUSIC AND EXOTICISM

Crossing the entire park of Queluz, some 115 metres from north to south, is a stream, the Ribeira de Jamor, which is now channelled as a canal. It was formerly known as the Great Lake (*Lago Grande*). The Canal is lined with panels of blue and white tiles, which carry a great diversity of pictures, including sea ports, departures of ships, towers, castles and landscapes, many of them taken from engravings, no doubt, as was the custom at the time. In 1756, João Antunes was paid to lay around fifty thousand tiles, of unknown origin. Between 1775 and 1776, Manuel da Costa Rosado also painted tiles for the Canal.

In the outer part, the tiles that cover the verandahs, including the seats, are multi-coloured, with elegant palace scenes and hunting themes, after engravings. In the central part of the Canal is a commemorative pattern, of coloured tiles in the form of the coats of arms of the Houses of Braganza and Orléans.

In 1900, on the orders of King Carlos and Queen Amelia, the entire scheme was restored by Pereira Cão (José Maria Pereira Júnior) and Carlos Alberto Nunes, whose signatures appear on several panels. Alongside the canal are blue and white ceramic pots, replicas of the originals made by the Fábrica do Rato that stand in the Hanging Garden.

On this spot used to stand the House of the Lake (*Casa do Lago*), probably a summer house, decorated with panels painted by Bruno José do Vale in the chinoiserie style. Two of these are still in existence. This building was also known as the Chinese House (*Casa Chinesa*) or the Music House (*Casa da Música*), because the Queen's chamber music was played here. On summer evenings, the 'Royal Personages' went by boat over the mirror-like water – trapped by a series of lock gates and reflecting the tiled designs. At night, lanterns in the form of carved, gilded cornucopiae were lit all along the waterway.

Tradition has it that there were mulberry bushes beside the road bordering the Canal, to boost the silk industry, which pleased the Marquis of Pombal, who was a keen supporter of national trade. The *Gazeta de Lisboa* of 7 June 1805 refers to the rearing of silkworms and silk spinning at Queluz by the Ladies of the Royal Household: 'Our Lady the Princess [Carlota Joaquina] continues to honour the New Establishment of the Royal Company, for the spinning and twisting of silks, informing all workers and keepers of this kind, that the Princess is rearing in the Royal Palace of Queluz and in her own room a large number of Silk Worms which are sometimes fed by her Royal Hands.'

The entire area of the Canal and the Robillion Staircase was a focus for Court entertainments, and was specially built with leisure and amusement in mind. Somewhere in this area was the '*Barraca Rica*', a

Above: Central portion of the Tiled Canal over the Ribeira do Jamor, former site of the Chinese or Music House.

Opposite: Interior of the Tiled Canal, seen from the east.

timber pavilion that served as a kind of country retreat for Royalty. It consisted of seven rooms, an entrance hall, a spare room, a coffee room, a state room and various private rooms. Completed in 1757, it was richly decorated with carving by Silvestre Faria Lobo. The walls were lined with damask and mirrored wall panels, according to a detailed description in a document prepared at the time of its appraisal by the architect Mateus Vicente de Oliveira.

Painted and gilded cages were made for this location by Silvestre Faria Lobo in 1759. Queen Maria I, Dona Carlota Joaquina and the Infantas kept birds in these, from the most common species, such as doves and canaries, to the more exotic cockatoos and eagles.

Beckford refers to these cages in 1794: 'The afternoon was drawing to a close and shadows were falling rapidly on the groves, the pavilion and the bird-cages; small lights shone in the distance, perhaps glow-worms, perhaps meteors.'

Before the departure of the Royal Family to Brazil, a colony of 183 black and white swans lived on the numerous lakes of Queluz. In the grounds surrounding the Palace were buffalo, deer, Angolan sheep and goats, as well as more common species. The cages built in 1822, below the Terrace of the Robillion Pavilion and by the Shell Waterfall (*Cascata das Conchas*) are reported still to have housed two lions, two tigers and various monkeys in 1833, evidence of an enduring taste for the exotic that is manifest on many levels in the house and gardens of the Palace.

Facing the wall that supported the Hanging Garden was the large Labyrinth Garden (*Jardim do Labirinto*), built during the 1760s, with its five lakes and coloured sculptures. Sadly these have now disappeared, but drawings of them feature in the plan of the gardens,

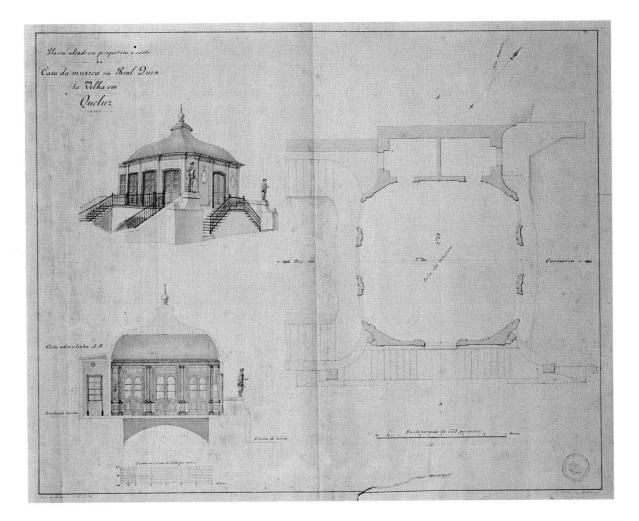

dating from the mid-eighteenth century, now lodged in Rio de Janeiro.

Walking to the end of the Canal, towards the brook, it is still possible to see the pitch for the Quoit or Ball Game (*Jogo da Malha ou da Bola*), which was played in Queluz from 1758. King José was a great enthusiast, in particular, as was his grandson Dom José, Prince of Brazil.

Of the other leisure pursuits that took place in this area, only the memory lives on: the Little Horses Game (*Jogo dos Cavalinhos*), referred to in 1754, involved an octagonal merry-go-round with glass doors and four painted wooden horses, surrounding a giant holding a lance; in the '*Jogo do Truque*' pavilion a kind of billiards was played with four ivory balls and wooden cues.

Above: The Music or Chinese House, over the Canal. Plan, section and perspective, in a watercolour pen drawing by an unknown artist, 2nd half of the 18th century. 500 x 620 mm. (Arq. Hist. do Ministério das Finanças/ANTT)

Opposite: The central portion of the Tiled Canal, from the east, in an oil painting by Carlos Alberto Nunes, signed and dated 1901. 990 x 690 mm. In the background is the former lock gate that retained the water, forming the so-called 'Great Lake'. (National Palace of Queluz)

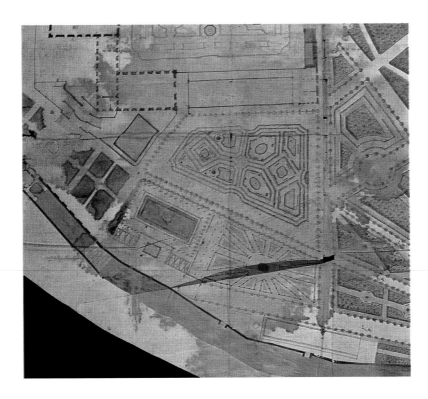

Above: The Shell Waterfall on the terrace of the Robillion Pavilion, overlooking the Tiled Canal.

Left: The Labyrinth Garden, shown in a plan of the mid-18th century.
(National Library of Rio de Janeiro)

Opposite: The Medals Lake, the largest lake in the Palace grounds, designed by Jean-Baptiste Robillion in 1764.

Following pages:
The Fountain of Neptune.

BROAD WALK OF THE LAKE OF MEDALS

In the northern part of the park, probably forming the main route from the former gardens of the Palace of the Marquises of Castelo Rodrigo, is the longest broad walk on the Queluz estate. It begins in the east, in a square dominated by a sculptural group in lead, which once crowned the façade of the Throne Room. The subject is *Samson Killing a Philistine*, in an interpretation by John Cheere, inspired by a marble original by Giambologna (1529–1608), now in the Victoria and Albert Museum in London.

This long broad walk comes to an end in the west at the Bulls' Corral Tank (*Tanque do Curro*), but is interrupted on its way by three large circular intersections, off which lead hedge-lined secondary paths forming the geometry of the garden. The first of these contains the largest piece of water in the gardens, known as the Lake of Medals, which was designed by the architect Robillion in 1764. The delicately conceived surrounding masonry is in the form of a star-shaped octagon, with the corners cut by small basins reminiscent of medals; it also has a complicated system of water jets. Bordering the lake are two lead statues representing Diana and Adonis.

A little further on, after passing a small slope which lends great harmony to the perspective of the broad walk, is an imposing group in stone, *Neptune Surrounded by Tritons*, sculpted by Ercole Ferrata (1610–1686), a pupil and assistant of Gianlorenzo Bernini.

Commissioned in 1677 for the Anunciada Palace by the second Count of Ericeira, it was finally erected in its present position, following various vicissitudes, in 1945, in a recently constructed lake.

BOTANICAL GARDEN

In 1769 work started on a Botanical Garden, which was completed in 1776. Until recently, it was situated at the lower end of the Estate, in a considerably altered form, in the site now occupied by the arena of the Portuguese School of Equestrian Art. It was bounded by balustrades erected in 1800. Also known as the Hothouse Garden (*Jardim das Estufas*), where King Pedro III planted pineapples, it was adorned with lakes and statues.

In addition to the pineapple hothouses, there was also a small Chinese pavilion, a kind of wooden folly, decorated with painted panels in the chinoiserie style by Bruno José do Vale. This stood between two hothouses and was kept for oriental plants. The setting was completed with a carved archway decorated with figures, and a small lake with lead sculptures.

As was the case in other European courts where the collecting of exotic species was fashionable, several members of the Portuguese Royal Family had an interest in botany. In 1765, the famous Italian naturalist Domenico Vandelli (1735–1816) supervised work on the Botanical Garden at Ajuda, designing another for the University of Coimbra some years later. He dedicated his *Dicionário de Termos Técnicos de História Natural, Memória sobre a Utilização dos Jardins Botânicos* (Dictionary of Technical Terms of Natural History, A Record of the Utilization of Botanic Gardens) to Queen Maria I and it is likely that she had been involved in the Botanical Garden at Queluz.

Carriages used to enter the park through the gate adjoining this garden, sadly unused nowadays because of the main road running past the Palace, or through the Ajuda Gate (*Portão da Ajuda*), which was commissioned by King João VI as a way to the palace of the same name. They would follow the broad walks, before stopping at the Robillion Staircase to enable their occupants to enter the Palace by the marble stairs that led to the Ambassadors' Hall.

Opposite Page: Detail of the Lake of Medals.

Left: Samson Killing a Philistine, *a lead sculpture, from John Cheere's London studio, 3rd quarter of the 18th century (formerly on top of the façade of the Throne Room).*

BULLFIGHTING AND EQUESTRIANISM

Equestrian arts, including jousting, the lively *Corrida ao Estafermo* (a feat of skill that consisted of spearing a spinning dummy without being caught by the whip it was brandishing) and bullfighting, were constantly practised at Queluz from the time of the Infante Dom Francisco.

In 1765 the construction of a relatively simple bull-ring was completed, with a sandy arena, a royal box, two small rooms where the Royal Family could rest or be greeted before the contest, and verandahs with iron railings. There was also a corral for bulls, which was then sited where the appropriately named Corral Tank (*Tanque do Curro*) still stands. This water source is functioning today.

In 1769, the *Rol dos Moços que foram com a obrigação de cavalaria para tourear em Queluz em o dia de S. Pedro* (List of Young Men who went to Queluz with the obligation of fighting bulls on St Peter's Day) contained forty names. During the first quarter of the nineteenth century, Queen Carlota Joaquina ordered the building of a bull-ring in the *Matinha* for the Infante Dom Miguel, who was a great bullfighting enthusiast and a distinguished horseman.

At the north-east end of the park, in a stable next to the Corral Tank, is the Portuguese School of Equestrian Art, where riders and Portuguese-bred Lusitanian horses from Alter can practise their skills. The school has been housed in the Palace grounds since 1995, continuing the tradition of royal horsemanship established by King João V in 1748. Some of the horses are stabled in the mews built early in the twentieth century on the orders of Queen Amélia.

Opposite: A knight running at the dummy, in an engraving taken from Luz da Liberal e Nobre Arte da Cavalaria, *by Manuel Carlos de Andrade, 1790.*

Right: Lunging reins in use at the Portuguese School of Equestrian Art.

Below: The interior of Queen Amelia's mews, commissioned in the early 20th century, in the French style.

BIBLIOGRAPHY

ABRANTES, Laura Junot, Duchesse d'. *Souvenirs d'une Ambassade et d'un Séjour en Espagne et en Portugal de 1808 a 1811*. Paris, 1837.

AFONSO, Simonetta Luz. *O Palácio de Queluz*. Publicações Alfa, 1986.

AFONSO, Simonetta Luz e DELAFORCE, Ângela. *Palácio de Queluz-Jardins*. Ed. IPPC/Quetzal, Lisboa, 1988.

ALVES, Artur da Mota. *Uma Festa no Palácio de Queluz em 1795*. Publicações dos Anais das Bibliotecas, Museus e Arquivos Históricos Municipais, Lisboa, 1935.

BECKFORD, William. *Italy with Sketches of Spain and Portugal (1787)*. London, 1834.

BECKFORD,William. *Recollections of an Excursion to the Monasteries of Alcobaça and Batalha*. London, 1838.

BECKFORD, William. *Diário de William Beckford em Portugal e Espanha*. Biblioteca Nacional, Lisboa, 2ª ed., 1983.

CÂNCIO, Francisco. *O Paço de Queluz*. Lisboa, 1950.

FRONTEIRA, Marquês da. *Memórias do Marquês da Fronteira e D'Alorna, D. José Trazimundo Mascarenhas Barreto*. Imprensa da Universidade, Coimbra, 1928.

GORANI, José. *Portugal, A Corte e o País nos anos de 1765 a 1767*. Tradução, prefácio e notas por Castelo Branco Chaves, Lisboa, 1945.

GOUVEIA, João Cândido Baptista. *Polícia Secreta dos Últimos Tempos do Reinado do Senhor Dom João VI*. Lisboa, 1835.

GUEDES, Natália Brito Correia. *O Palácio dos Senhores do Infantado em Queluz*. Livros Horizonte, Lisboa, 1971.

LICHNOWSKY, Príncipe Félix. *Portugal, Recordações do Ano de 1842*. Prefácio e notas por Castelo Branco Chaves, Lisboa, 1946.

MACHADO, Cyrillo Volkmar. *Colecção de Memórias relativas às vidas dos Pintores e escultores, architectos e gravadores portugueses e dos estrangeiros que estiverão em Portugal*. Lisboa, 1823.

PIRES, António Caldeira. *História do Palácio Nacional de Queluz*. 2 vols., Coimbra, 1925-1926.

PORFÍRIO, António Ventura. "O Palácio Nacional de Queluz Restaurado" Revista Ocidente, vol. XII, nº 34, Lisboa, 1941.

RESENDE, Marquês de. "Descripção e Recordações históricas do Paço e Quinta de Queluz", in Panorama, vols XI, XII e XIV, Lisboa, 1854-1857.

TWISS, Richard. *Travels through Portugal and Spain in 1772 and 1773*. London, 1775.

WORDSWORTH, Dora. *Journal of a few months residence in Portugal*. London, 1847.

Estatuária de Chumbo. "Palácio de Queluz", in *Boletim da Direcção-Geral dos Edifícios e Monumentos Nacionais*, nº110, Lisboa, 1962.

D. Pedro d'Alcântara de Bragança 1798-1834. Catálogo de exposição, Palácio Nacional de Queluz, 1986.

No 2º Centenário da Morte do Príncipe D. José. Catálogo de exposição, Sociedade de Estudos do Século XVIII e Palácio Nacional de Queluz, 1988.

William Beckford e Portugal. Catálogo de exposição, Palácio Nacional de Queluz, 1987.

FONTES MANUSCRITAS – ARQUIVOS: Academia Nacional de Belas Artes, Arquivo Nacional da Torre do Tombo (A.N.T.T.), Biblioteca da Ajuda, Biblioteca Nacional de Lisboa, Biblioteca Nacional do Rio de Janeiro e Direcção Geral dos Edifícios e Monumentos Nacionais. (DGEMN)

INDEX